A
Warwickshire
Christmas

A
Warwickshire
Christmas

Compiled by David Green

ALAN SUTTON

First published in the United Kingdom in 1990
Alan Sutton Publishing Limited · Phoenix Mill ·
Far Thrupp · Stroud · Gloucestershire

First published in the United States of America in 1991
Alan Sutton Publishing Inc. · Wolfeboro Falls ·
NH 03896–0848

British Library Cataloguing in Publication Data

A Warwickshire Christmas.
1. Anthologies in English
I. Green, David
082

ISBN 0–86299–766–6

Library of Congress Cataloging in Publication Data
applied for

Cover illustration: detail from Christmas comes but once a year!
Pears' print, anon, 1896. (Fine Art Photographic Library
Limited.)

Typeset in Garamond 12/13
Typesetting and origination by
Alan Sutton Publishing Limited
Printed in Great Britain by
Dotesios Printers Ltd, Trowbridge, Wiltshire.

Contents

· A Warwickshire Christmas ·

· A Warwickshire Christmas ·

vii

· A Warwickshire Christmas ·

Once Upon a Christmas

URSULA BLOOM

Ursula Bloom, the Warwickshire writer who died in 1984 at the age of ninety-one, gained a place in The Guinness Book of Records *as the authoress who has written the greatest number of published books — 560 in all. Much of her childhood was spent in the village of Whitchurch, where her father was rector, and it was from that period of her life that some of her most evocative Christmas recollections were recorded. In this first selection, she looks back on some of the festive customs she cherished most from those early days.*

Yuletide or Christ's Mass has gone through the centuries as the great feast of the year, and the little hamlets of Warwickshire kept it joyously in their own way, with mummers and parties of carollers who journeyed from house to house. Today their carols are the accepted ones; once they were of the county, like the one the village men from Ilmington used to sing:

> In comes I, old mother Christmas,
> Welcome or welcome not.
> I hope old mother Christmas
> Will ne-er be forgot.

'The carol singers came and sang . . .'

In the old days, and even at the start of the century, the houses were decorated mostly with holly, which filled the windows so that it would show from the outside. In Stow-on-the-Wold, the villagers used ivy and bay as well, and 'whatsoever is green'. Later when mistletoe came in, it was considered most unlucky ever to take it down. It was said to preserve the house against fire, and could only be removed when a fresh lot was brought in. In the rectory at Whitchurch,

where I lived, our mistletoe stayed stuck up in an old broken lantern all the year round, and uncommonly dusty it became.

St Thomas's Day, the 21st December, was fixed for the widows of the parishes to go 'Thomasing', or 'Mumping' as it is known in Norfolk. Kindly folk in the big houses dispensed refreshments, and many of the widows spent the night in a frosty ditch, coming-to!

At Tredington, at the end of the last century, only the children collected for the widows, and at Halford the young-sters were given a half-holiday for this purpose. Church bells rang to mark the day.

Christmas meant a lot of work at our rectory, and much cogitation with the patron of the living, James Roberts-West, of Alscot Park. Although Squire Roberts-West was seldom there himself, his charming wife, of whom I was very fond, helped with the charities, and Christmas came top of the list. There was the day of what was known as 'The Gifts' when the local women went to collect their due. A list was kept (edited by my mother) showing what they had received the previous year, and this influenced what they should now be given.

The 'gifts' consisted of a pair of blankets, or perhaps sheets. They might also have been 'the Bundles', which contained yards of flannel and a honeycomb quilt, or two pillow slips, bolster case, and some yards of sheeting.

Bread and meat were doled out at this festival, a loaf of bread for each member of the household over a year old, and also a pound of meat. Some of the very old people received coal, for our village was entitled to it, being one of the four on the Roberts-West estate.

We also had to cope with the Ayscough charity. At one time the Ayscoughs had lived there, and had left to every widow and widower in the parish, a certain income which was divided among them at Christmas. Many of them prayed for a bad November, which would, perhaps, remove a couple, and mean

3

more for those left. One always felt that God had been particularly unkind if one of them died immediately *after* Christmas. 'He had ought to ha' done that thair a'fore', the others commented.

At the rectory we decorated gaily, and the first real excitement began on Christmas Eve when the footman from Alscot Park arrived with our personal gifts. The parents got such dull things – strange-looking bottles, a hare, a brace of pheasants, or a turkey. The children, however, were most generously treated. The maids, too, had their thrill, for the gifts were brought by an extremely good-looking young footman, known affectionately among them as 'The Cock Sparrow'. He looked very handsome in the West uniform.

My father cycled into Stratford to bring back ten shillings' worth of coppers for carollers, from the bank, and a load of halfpenny yellowish oranges for the children. Then we were properly prepared for the great day.

The children did not attend early service, but got busy with their stockings. In those days one did not dispute the reality of an old man called Father Christmas or Santa Claus. I remember I had a theory that he was Jesus Christ 'dressed up', and this was just another of his very kindly acts. At eleven there was a big service at church with a procession to 'Christians Awake'. My father, in his wild enthusiasm, would have the choir walk with him, singing round the church itself, stumbling about a frozen or muddy churchyard.

We returned to a very ordinary lunch, to be followed by the excitement of the Christmas tree. Then came the arranging of the dessert for the one enormous dinner of the year, with myself prodding crackers with a small fat finger, and trying to get some idea of what might be inside them.

All through this state dinner, with the special table-centre (a most hideous scarlet and silver thing that my mother had made specially for this night), the carol singers came and sang,

and one was constantly rushing out with coppers and yellow oranges. My mother was usually in a frenzy lest 'the children will catch their death'.

Boxing morning was also a big occasion. At eleven o'clock the Newbold Brass Band arrived, marching in to 'Whilst Shepherds Watched', and setting the echoes ringing. Hot cocoa and mince pies awaited them. They would be followed by the handbell ringers, who came into the hall, and stood there clanging out 'Hark the Herald Angels Sing'. (More hot cocoa and mince pies.) There was always a tremendous thrill in the kitchen, where they all went to eat their refreshments. The thrill was increased because the skittish ones had mistletoe attached to their caps.

After cold turkey for Boxing Day lunch, we would walk to Alscot Park to say thank you for our gifts. All the four parsons' families did that, armed with lanterns, and often falling over browsing deer or sleeping cows, as they came back after dark.

There were also parties given to the village, as well as to us. Warwick Castle's was a delightful one, and it meant a ride in a hired fly (at vast cost, we felt), in which we sat getting colder and colder, huddled in shawls, and with the tin footwarmer chilling in the straw at our feet. But how wonderful Warwick looked with its Christmas garlands, and its quite enormous Christmas tree. All that was the goodness of the beautiful and adorable Lady Warwick, who had so generous a heart that the estate has never quite forgotten it.

One year the Shirleys of nearby Ettington gave a children's party, and were terribly modern about it, for they engaged what was then called 'the Bioscope', from the Coliseum in London, to give a performance. I remember I had not a clue what it was all about, because it flickered so dreadfully.

Christmas was certainly a great festival for the children, and an exciting one for the village. Everybody got a bit more than they had expected to get. The rectory door was open to any

guest, for we had much to share. I remember once hearing my
uncle from Ireland saying to my father: 'The awful thing is,
that it's bound to happen all over again next year, isn't it?' I
thought he had gone mad.

The time came in my childhood, as it does to all of us, when
in the sanctuary of the butler's pantry, I asked a chatty
parlourmaid: 'Is Father Christmas really true?' She gave me the
equivalent of the horny eye, suspecting my motives probably.
Then with supreme caution she said: 'Maybe he be, maybe he
b'aint, but we just takes what he bring along of him, and no
one don't ask silly questions'.

An Army
Christmas, 1940

VIVIAN BIRD

*A prolific and versatile writer, with numerous books and
countless column-inches in newspapers and magazines to
his credit, Vivian Bird possesses a deep and incisive
knowledge of his native Warwickshire, a county for which
he has always had a special regard. Here he recalls a
wartime Christmas, the rigours of which were hardly
mollified by the fact that the army unit with which he was
serving, was stationed only a few miles from his home.*

· *A Warwickshire Christmas* ·

Christmas Day 1940 began tragically for the fieldmouse, though I felt no little sorrow myself. After all, it had spent the night with me in my blankets. I first felt it wriggle when I had become too warm and comfortable to contemplate evicting it, and as I had done a 10 p.m. to midnight guard duty on Christmas Eve, I could enjoy the luxury of a long kip.

Now, as I shook out my blankets, my tiny bedfellow was summarily despatched by Jeff Coleman's army boot.

The bell tent which Jeff and I shared was in the corner of a field at Pathlow, off the A34, north of Stratford-upon-Avon. The angle of a couple of hedges afforded protection from the winter winds, and a nearby cow pond provided ablution facilities which by January, when the pond was ice-bound, became almost impossible. But on Christmas morning I experienced no difficulty, though scant comfort, in washing and shaving.

Walking up the field to the cookhouse and the huts, I called in at the sentry-box-type toilet. Some days later when the snow came, I was to be subjected to my fellow-gunners' humour in that same place of refuge, as they secured the door from the outside and shovelled snow through the gap between it and the roof until I was chest deep.

It is an army custom that on Christmas Day the officers wait on the men. Our Christmas dinner had been laid on at the Navigation Inn at Wootton Wawen, and we wanted for nothing. Before and after the meal, sycophantic gunners kept buying the popular troop officer whiskies beyond even his capacity, so that he surreptitiously 'forgot' them on any convenient mantelpiece or window sill. My friend Jim later told me that I followed the troop officer round and drained each jettisoned glass. Even so, I was one of few sober soldiers piling into the three-ton truck which took us back to the searchlight site in time for the customary 'Stand To' at dusk.

The thin khaki line numbering off is one of my most

hilarious memories of five years' war service, as it buckled and broke as the men staggered this way and that, or fell flat on their faces. It was just as well that manning the equipment was dispensed with on that particular night. The searchlight would probably have accomplished as zigzag a course skyward as the soldiers in that 'Stand To' line on the ground.

So the rest of the evening was free, except for guard duty, and Jim expressed an urgent need to cycle to the Golden Cross at Bearley at the bottom of Pathlow Hill. Fearing that he would have sustained grievous harm, I wrestled with him among our equipment, and though giving away a couple of stone and several gallons of alcohol, I managed to dissuade him.

So he repaired instead to his sleeping hut, the beds already occupied by several recumbent forms, and there he produced a bottle of whisky. 'I didn't so much buy it as come by it,' he said in answer to my enquiry. For a while it seemed to put him to sleep, until suddenly – perhaps with some fuddled memory of his days as an excellent hooker for Camp Hill Old Edwardians – he shot out a long leg and kicked over the red-hot stove. The stove pipe fell out of the roof, mercifully missing everybody, but burning coals flew on to the bed where George Wood was sleeping off the day's indulgence.

As we scrambled about trying to remove the smouldering blankets a drowsy George murmured 'Turn it in chaps'.

From such confusion I went to see my more sober friend Arthur Webb. Arthur, in charge of the searchlight generator, was exiled to a red barn where the generator noise would not interrupt orders when it was in action on the site. In that barn, among the hay bales and the rats, we shared a quiet midnight repast of poetry and mince pies. The barn still stands, isolated in the fields at Pathlow, and as I drive past on the Stratford road it enshrines my memories of Arthur, who died some years ago in Pembrokeshire, but whose memorial stone is in the churchyard at Temple Balsall in his native Warwickshire.

8

Although the field at Pathlow was our immediate home, our Troop headquarters were at nearby Edstone Hall, the fifth of its line to occupy the site since the reign of Charles I. The owner, Percy Pritchard, who now shared his home with the British army, had a daughter Beryl, and it was from her that our headquarters personnel received a delightful invitation to a festive party at the Hall in that bleak 1940 December.

Hand-written, and illustrated with an extraordinary assortment of sketches (one of the more incongruous depicting a camel under a palm tree), it is still among my treasured possessions from those far-off wartime days.

It was headed 20.12.40, and read:

> Edstone Hall invites you all
> To a hearty Christmas party.
> So make yourselves all neat and tidy
> And come along at six on Friday.
> We hope that you'll enjoy the fun
> And forget the horrid nasty Hun.

Unfortunately I wasn't among the partygoers, but I seem to recall that for those lucky enough to attend, it was a memorable occasion.

from

Country Calendar

GODFREY BASELEY

Born in 1904, Godfrey Baseley is an acknowledged authority on the countryside and rural life. He became involved with farming programmes broadcast from the BBC's Birmingham studios after the Second World War, and in 1950 he created what is now a national institution, the radio serial The Archers. *Among his books is a delightful chronicle of rural life entitled* Country Calendar, *a month-by-month commentary on the countryside seen through the eyes of his friend Tom Artwright, a dedicated gamekeeper, and as applicable to Warwickshire as any of the Midland counties. This extract comes from the chapter for the month of December.*

As the month moved on towards Christmas the winds shifted from the northerly direction, where they had stayed for most of the first week, to a more westerly direction bringing milder weather, mists and some rain. The ponds that had been dry for so long were seen to be holding water once again, and here and there small pools lay in the ditches. There was no water though to be seen flowing through the drainage pipes where they emptied themselves into the ditches.

'It'll take a heavy fall of snow and a slow thaw afore we shall

see them flowing again,' was Tom's comment. 'It's a long time since I saw ground so dry at this time of the year. It certainly looks as though we are leading up to a "green" Christmas, and you knows what they says about that, don't you? A green Christmas and a full churchyard.'

It was a green Christmas, and for several days before, the whole of the countryside was enveloped in a thick mist. For a short time each day the pale winter sun was able to break through to cast long ghostlike shadows from the bare trees.

Although the invasion of the fieldfares had seemed to strip all the district bare of berries, bunches of mistletoe and branches of holly both bearing berries began to appear.

In the village, Christmas trees could be seen in the windows of the cottages and from the coloured fairy lights that formed an important part of their decoration, shafts of multi-coloured light pierced the darkness to light up and be absorbed by the enveloping mist.

In the Bull the decorations had gone up to hide the tobacco-stained walls and ceiling. Extra supplies of drinks and fancy packs of cigarettes lined the shelves behind the bar, and on the night of the annual Christmas draw the whole place was crowded to capacity, each one hopeful of taking home some of the top prizes that had tempted them to subscribe.

During the days before Christmas, the 'dark' days, Tom had made his annual round to deliver presents of a brace of pheasants to the tenant farmers and all who had in any way contributed to the success of the shooting season. Among these was the roadman, now retired, who for so many years had kept a watchful eye open for anything untoward that might have happened to the game.

'The number of folks to call on gets less every year. At one time there were over forty tenants on the estate, now there's only twelve. Over the years as the old ones have died out, the farms have either been brought into hand or have been

11

amalgamated with their neighbours. I can slip round them all in a couple of evenings in my Land Rover. When I first had the job to do, I used to go around in a horse and float, with the birds that the squire had helped to select and label, laid out on a bed of straw in the bottom of the float.

'You was always welcome, too welcome sometimes, and I must admit that there were a few occasions when I was glad that the old horse knew his way home.

'Christmas was quite a time at the Manor in the old days. Apart from preparing for the big house parties that they usually had, there was parcels of groceries to be packed up and delivered to every house where the people worked on the estate. Very practical parcels they were. Tea, sugar, cheese, butter and all that sort of thing. Most of these parcels were delivered personally by her ladyship who was driven round the village by the coachman, with a footman to carry the parcels.

'You know, it is strange to think that that all happened within my memory. What a change I have seen in my lifetime so far. Goodness knows what is still to come.'

Christmas as it Was

TED BALDWIN

*In the Hockley district of Birmingham, the festive season,
for most children, somehow had a special air of magic
about it during the years of depression between the wars.
The celebrations, of necessity, may have been more humble
than those of today, but they were sincere and exciting and
– as Ted Baldwin recalls – unforgettable.*

Christmastime in the 1920s and 1930s was heralded with the
same joy and enthusiasm as always, in spite of those years of
depresssion and much unemployment. People, as at any time,
seemed to find money from somewhere to buy a few presents
for their children, but at what sacrifice I can only guess. The
Star of Bethlehem shone no less brightly over our humble
street in the Hockley district of Birmingham, than anywhere
else.

When Christmas was still a few weeks ahead, it always
seemed an age arriving, but as the great day drew near, so the
feeling of anticipation increased. The preparations carried
perhaps a greater degree of excitement than Christmas Day
itself.

The contribution of many boys and girls in those days was
to provide the decorative trimmings. With sheets of coloured
paper, a twopenny bottle of glue, a paintbrush and a pair of
scissors, we made paper-chains that were hung round the walls
and over the pictures in our main room. Behind the pictures,

13

A wintry scene at Five Ways, Birmingham, around the time
of the First World War

we most likely placed sprigs of holly or mistletoe, which were
quite cheap in those days. Christmas trees were rarely seen in
the homes of the poorer areas of Birmingham.

Then there were trips into the city centre by tram to enjoy
the sights. One of the scenes I can still recollect was what
might well have been the first time an illuminated Father
Christmas appeared on the front of Lewis's building. In the
street outside, crowds of people stood tightly packed, gazing
up in awe.

A large number of people with children could also be seen
waiting by the clock in Market Hall for the little figures on the
platform to move into position to strike the bells at the
appointed time. The clock, alas, fell a victim to bombs in
1940.

Before the age of indoor ready-made entertainment arrived, children could go out and enjoy simple Christmas sights such as these, and it hardly seemed to matter if it happened to be cold or raining.

I remember too our visits to Birmingham's Great Western Arcade, also damaged by enemy bombs in the war. Situated off Colmore Row it had a large arched glass roof, and steps led to the balcony on which, at Christmastide, a section was converted by green and grey papier-mâché into a make-believe cave. Through this we came to a grotto where, in the dull red-lit interior, we met Father Christmas and obtained our sixpenny dip.

Afterwards, mingling with the crowds of people, many of whom were carrying presents, we began our journey home, pausing here and there to gaze in shop windows and at the spectacular Christmas illuminations in the city centre.

On Christmas Eve, some people stayed in the Market Hall until quite late, to seek out bargains as the poultry prices dropped. In those days, before battery-produced poultry came into being, it was the only time of the year that most of us ate fowl of any kind.

The school Christmas party was always a real treat for youngsters, particularly as for some of them, it was the nearest they were ever likely to get to any sort of Christmas cheer. At the end of the party, each child was presented with a bag of sweets and an orange as we filed out of school to go home.

As carol singers we were as traditionally early in those days as the youngsters are today – and, I may add, just as intent on making a copper or two rather than heralding the season in the truly festive fashion.

There would be a shuffling of feet and a preliminary bout of giggles before faltering through the first few bars of 'Good King Wenceslas', and galloping through the rest of it. Then, anxious to get the whole thing over with, we ended with the

· *A Warwickshire Christmas* ·

'Faltering through the first few bars of "Good King Wenceslas" . . .'

usual 'Apples to eat and nuts to crack'. On Christmas Day itself, of course, the majority of us were far too busy enjoying our festive fare to turn out to sing carols on what was, after all, the proper day.

Most of us will also remember our parents advising us to go to bed early so that we would be fast asleep before Father Christmas arrived. But how hard we tried to stay awake. Then there was the thrill of waking during the early hours of Christmas morning, and noticing objects nearby which were merely shapes. And how we lay there presumably pondering

16

what they might be until, unable to contain ourselves any longer, we began to explore.

Later, if our parents were so inclined, a candle was lit, and they too shared our pleasure and perhaps thought that it was all worthwhile after all.

The Christmas stocking hanging at the foot of the bed was most likely one of Dad's socks, and contained the usual nuts, apples and oranges with maybe one or two paper-covered chocolate novelties.

Some of the more fortunate boys received Meccano sets, from which it was possible to make cranes that really worked, and many other things that ingenuity suggested. Or there might be one of those beautifully bound illustrated annuals of a favourite comic, like *Playbox*, *Tiger Tim's Weekly* or *Chatterbox*.

The Christmas days I recall were usually dull and mild, and rarely do I remember snow falling. During the morning we youngsters went outside to show off our presents to each other. One or two of us perhaps had Cowboy or Indian outfits, and six-shooters filled with caps would be heard cracking here and there in the street. The girls would be showing off their new dolls.

Soon, however, early darkness fell and the streets became strangely quiet for the rest of the day and into the evening.

Despite all the changes which have come about since those days, Christmas still remains a time of festivity. On the other hand, some of the traditional customs of New Year's Eve no longer seem in evidence.

In the late 'twenties and early 'thirties, at the stroke of midnight on New Year's Eve, the air was filled with sounds. Church bells rang out, as they, at least, still do today. Steam locomotives blew their whistles, and the factory sirens which daily summoned people to work and dismissed them at night, now had a more joyful meaning as, in varying degrees of pitch, they jointly sustained their sounds. Railway maroons were set off too, and the noise resembled gun fire.

17

Meanwhile, doors in every street opened and neighbours greeted one another with the cry: 'Happy New Year'. Children too, late as it was, ran along the street opening doors and calling the same greeting. Older boys and girls followed them crying out: 'Let the New Year in . . . let the New Year in'.

If a person had black hair, he or she would be welcome to come in at the front door and leave at the back. It was a sign of good luck for the coming year, and anyone performing this generous act was awarded a sixpence according to custom. Another tradition was to present neighbours with a piece of coal as a symbol to ward off want in the coming year.

The streets soon cleared, and in sharp contrast to the noise of celebration, they quickly returned to the silence of the night, and to the beginning of a new year.

We were all full of hope in those days: hope for better times ahead.

from

Life's Ebb and Flow

FRANCES, COUNTESS OF WARWICK

In the last years of Victoria's reign and during the early years of the present century, Frances, Countess of Warwick, was a formidable character in the life of the county,

18

and a hostess of almost limitless generosity. But as these extracts from her autobiography show, her dazzling public activities were increasingly tempered by a growing aware-ness of the principles of Socialism which were later to play so important a part in her life. The first passage, which she quotes from a contemporary newspaper report, describes a Christmas ball at her estate in Essex.

'On Boxing Day the Countess of Warwick invited the whole of the employees on her Easton Lodge Estate and the village school children to a Christmas tree party at the Lodge. The

Frances, Countess of Warwick, photographed around the turn of the century

19

handsome ballroom was used for the last time before being removed to Warwick Castle, and spacious though it is, the company filled it. In the centre was a large fir tree, taken out of the park, and reaching from the floor to the ceiling. Many hundreds of toys, of all imaginable descriptions, together with a number of sparkling brilliants, were hung upon the tree; in fact the tree was so laden that its foliage could scarcely be seen.

'Around this huge and glistening Christmas tree were arranged a number of electric-light chandeliers. Along each side of the ballroom there were tables covered with useful articles to be given away. There were handsome fur-lined coats for the principal household servants, jewellery or trinkets for others, packages of toys, all of a costly description, for every child, fancy articles of dress or warm clothing for other servants, while for every man who works in the grounds at Easton there was a red woollen jersey. On a separate table was a collection of silverware and jewellery, which the Countess had provided for each member of her house-party.

'At five o'clock the household servants, numbering fifty, left their duties in order to range themselves on either side of the ballroom, and then the village children were ushered in. Well might the little ones falter on entering, for the ballroom, with its white walls and Corinthian pillars, blue ceiling, and gilt chairs, was ablaze with electric light, and the scene was one which will long be remembered by all who witnessed it.

'The Rector of Little Easton, the Revd A.L. Whitfield, quickly stepped forward to take the children in hand, and the Countess made her visitors feel at home at once. Behind the children entered one hundred outside workmen – game-keepers, woodmen, gardeners, estate artisans, stablemen, motor-men, etc. The Earl and Countess of Warwick had a pleasant welcome from everybody, and Lord Brooke walked in in shooting costume. Lady Marjorie Greville assisted her mother in the distribution of the presents.

· A Warwickshire Christmas ·

'The Countess of Warwick wore a beautiful dress by Doucet of Paris. It was composed of delicately painted muslin, trimmed with fur and turquoise velvet, and spotted over with little diamond buckles. The dress had a lace front, also trimmed round with fur and turquoise velvet, and marked with diamond buckles. Round her waist her ladyship wore a blue silk sash. She had a black picture hat. Lady Marjorie Greville wore a blue accordian-pleated crêpe de Chine frock, trimmed with fur, with a blue hat.

'When the packages had been distributed, the little son of the Earl and Countess, the Hon Maynard Greville, entered the ballroom perched on the broad shoulders of his brother, Lord Brooke, and from this position he began stripping the Christmas tree, giving the toys to the children. The little boy, who greatly enjoyed the gathering, was dressed in a pale blue suit, with white collar. At the close, cheer after cheer was raised for the Earl and Countess and their family.'

I have given this description in full because today I believe this is the wrong method of giving! It is a mistaken benevolence, an echo of our feudal past. The new order will lay emphasis on co-operation in work and wealth, instead of sharpening the contrast between the rich giver and the poor receiver.

On another occasion the Countess organized a lavish winter ball at Warwick Castle.

There was to be revelry in the Castle, but ten weeks of black frost had seen to it that hunger and want were the portion of many cottage homes. It was the cruelly hard winter of 1895, the year after I entered Warwick Castle as its chatelaine, the death of old Lord Warwick, my father-in-law, in 1894, having made my husband successor to the title. The year's mourning was over, and my plans for the house-warming celebrations

included a fancy-dress ball – then something of a novelty – on a splendidly lavish scale.

Dancing was to be in the Cedar Drawing Room, which is panelled with Vandykes. The fashion and beauty of London and the county gathered for pleasure. Neighbours had house-parties, and the whole district was filled with the bustle of preparation. The ball was spoken of as 'the event of the winter'.

Meanwhile, I heard continually of great distress among the poor. Work had stopped altogether in the building and auxiliary trades, and while working-class earnings were at their lowest, the need for food and clothing and fuel grew more and more intense. While my sympathies were roused by the dark side of the picture, I felt happy in the belief that our ball was giving work to so many people who would otherwise have been idle. The festivities of the Lords and Ladies Bountiful were being translated into terms of meat and bread for the workers, and this thought allayed my troubled inward feelings.

The Castle was overflowing with guests. The principal colour scheme for the occasion was white and gold, and as it was winter, masses of arum lilies and lilies of the valley were got from the Riviera. The gold drawing-room was lit by wax candles and electric light. A few names stand out among the large house-party. Prince Francis of Teck. M. de Soveral, Count Deym, Princess Henry of Pless, the then Miss Cornwallis West, the Duchess of Sutherland, Lady Norreys, the Duke of Marlborough, Lord Chesterfield, Lord Grey de Wilton, and many others. Various guests brought parties with them by special trains, and the effect of the throng of splendidly gowned and costumed men and women in the setting of the noble rooms of the Castle seemed at the time to make the gathering worthwhile. It was a novelty in those days to provide a photographing room, and the results proved its great success.

22

· A Warwickshire Christmas ·

There may be readers who will be interested to learn that my ball-gown was of turquoise velvet brocade, embroidered with genuine gold thread in fleur-de-lis and roses. Diamond tiaras clasped the shoulders and my head-dress was made of tissue of gold with a rivière of diamonds, while plumes of pink, white and blue were fastened by star sapphires set with diamonds. I was supposed to be impersonating Queen Marie Antoinette.

The success of the Countess of Warwick's flamboyant entertaining was universally acknowledged, and her circle of friends stretched to many countries. At Christmas in 1897, two years after the great party at Warwick Castle, she received these felicitations from an Indian 'holy man' who was evidently one of her admirers.

Sharpura,
Rajputana,
India,

25.12.97.

Dear Lady Warwick,
   I wish you from the core of my heart a happy Xmas and pray that the New Year be joyful to you.
Yours ever sincerely,

SINGH RAJKUMAR.

Post Haste!

VIC ROGERS

Coaching inns and stage coaches set against snowy landscapes are still favourite, if anachronistic, subjects for our modern-day Christmas cards. But in the severe winter of 1836, they were very much a part of day-to-day life in snowbound Warwickshire. Vic Rogers, chronicler of many aspects of local history, wrote this graphic account in 1977.

In keeping with the festive spirit, the Christmas card robins are plump and well-fed, and under the skilled hands of the jovial coachman the team of sleek horses makes little effort of hauling the stage coach full of elegant passengers over the powdery snow. In real life, the robins are less than their exaggerated portraits imply, and travelling by stage coach was an adventure not to be undertaken lightly.

The heyday of coaching was marked by many harsh winters, and the snowstorms over the Christmas period of 1836 were particularly savage. The *Coventry Standard* of Friday, 30th December, informed those who handed over their 4½d., that the severity of the weather 'has been extraordinary in the last week. On Saturday, Sunday and Monday night the wind blew with great violence and the fall of snow (especially on the Sunday) has been tremendous. We believe such a rapid accumulation and such a sudden stoppage on the roads has not been known for these twenty years.

· A Warwickshire Christmas ·

'The principal stoppage appears to have been on the road between Weedon and Dunchurch. Several hundred men have been employed to clear away the snow, and now have so far succeeded so that the mails carrying two days' papers and letters arrived in this city yesterday morning. The Rein Deer which left London on Wednesday evening at seven o'clock arrived about three in the afternoon of yesterday . . .'

That particular Sunday when the fall of snow was so heavy, was, in fact, Christmas Day, but by then the mail coaches to London had already been brought to a stop at Dunchurch, near Rugby, and the passengers given accommodation at the Dun Cow and the Green Man.

Many of the travellers had intended to be with their families in London for the Yuletide, and in normal conditions their journey to the Bull and Mouth, near the new Post Office in St Martin's le Grand, would have been completed in good time. Indeed, there were two Coventry stage-coach operators who advertised that their 'new and elegant' post coach, The Ruby, would cover the ninety-odd miles from High Street, Coventry, to the Bull and Mouth 'in nine hours certain'. (If you think that a bull and a mouth make an unusual inn-sign combination, the pairing originates from the corruption of Boulogne Mouth, the location of a battle against the French many years before.)

At that particular Christmastime, the stranded passengers were disappointed at not being able to continue their journey and be home for the holiday, but things might have been much worse and at least they were warm and dry. In the evening a party was held at the Dun Cow, and the recent acquaintances were renewed.

It was usual at the start of a trip for the passengers to appoint a spokesman to act on their behalf with the coachman, and so introductions had already been made and then furthered as the coaches had headed south. The exceptionally bad

· A Warwickshire Christmas ·

With its 'outsiders' well wrapped up against the cold, the
Birmingham Post stage coach stops at the Quinton toll-gate
early in the last century

weather conditions also must have helped to foster the air of
bonhomie – albeit within two distinct groups: those able to
afford to travel inside, and the less affluent 'outsiders'.

The moneyed passengers travelling inside the coach would
take their places with decorum inside the inn yard, but
because of the height of the vehicle, the outsiders could only
climb aboard when the coach had negotiated the comparatively
low entry and stood ready on the road. The term 'outsider'
therefore, had a double application, referring both to boarding
and travelling outside, and quite rightly these passengers paid
a lower fare – reduced by about a half in the early 1800s.

· *A Warwickshire Christmas* ·

As if the loss of dignity, exposure to the elements and the danger of being the most likely to get hurt in the event of a mishap was not enough, one lady discovered there was even more, as this newspaper account recalls:

'On Tuesday last, a young woman who had lived as a servant in St Albans, came up to Coventry by the Northampton coach. On the road near Barnet, two fellows climbed behind the coach, and on the coachman threatening to apply his whip to their backs, they got down. On her arrival in Coventry she discovered the villains had cut through her gown and pocket and abstracted seven sovereigns, a half sovereign and ten shillings, leaving her only sixpence.'

The conversations that snowy evening between the dances at the Dun Cow will have to be imagined, but it is reasonable to suppose that the many aspects of travelling by coach were not neglected.

Thankfully there were some lighter moments to soften the winter hardships, and a popular contemporary anecdote concerned the passenger travelling inside a fully loaded coach. One of the passengers was very tall and his long legs made the journey somewhat uncomfortable for the poor man sitting opposite. For many miles the uneven sharing of the restricted space continued until, at the end of one stage, the tall man announced he was going out to stretch his legs. 'Oh God no,' cried the cramped passenger. 'They are far too long already.'

To round off their enforced stay in Dunchurch, the coachmen and passengers arranged for a shoot for the Boxing Day, and one hare apparently met an untimely end. Afterwards, the records tell us that they went along the Rugby road singing a selection of carols, and were rewarded by the local farmers with elderberry wine and pork pie. Perhaps this proffered friendship made some of the travellers feel a little less like outsiders during that wintry Christmas – which is not a bad thought at any time of the year.

27

from

The Country Diary of an Edwardian Lady

EDITH HOLDEN

Edith Holden's celebrated Country Diary *has become almost a cult since it was first published in 1977. She was born at King's Norton in 1871, and for much of her life she lived with her family in Olton near Solihull. It was the surrounding Warwickshire countryside which inspired her diary and gave her so much pleasure. In 1920, in her forty-ninth year, she died tragically by drowning in the Thames at Kew, while trying to collect buds from a chestnut tree. These few entries from her diary – including one of the many verses she quoted – were made over the Christmas period in 1906, and they well illustrate her deep awareness of the natural world.*

Dec. 1. Very bright and clear with a cold wind from the north-east. For many weeks past the birds have been coming to be fed in the mornings. Today I put out a cocoa-nut – to the great joy of the

Snow mantles the landscape near Solihull, a scene near
Edith Holden's former home at Olton

tom-tits; numbers of them were pecking away at it
all through the day — mostly blue-tits.

4. Three days of rain, wind and sunshine.

7. Hard white frost and fog. This is the first real
winter's day we have had. Crowds of birds came to
be fed this morning. There were great battles
among the tits over the cocoa-nut; and once a
robin got right into it and refused to let the tits
approach, until he had had all he wanted. I don't
think the robins really care for cocoa-nut, but they
don't like to see the tits enjoying anything,
without claiming a share.

29

9. We woke up to a storm of whirling snowflakes this morning — the first snow this winter. The storm was soon over however and it was followed by bright sunshine and a sharp frost at night.

10. Cold, frosty day. It seems as if winter had begun in earnest, but the forecasts prophesy a speedy change.

12. Wind and rain with bright intervals. There was a most beautiful rainbow visible in the morning for about ten minutes.

14. Heavy fall of snow.

20. After a rapid thaw and four days of wonderfully mild, still weather, without wind or rain, the wind has gone round to the east and it looks as if we might have a frosty Christmas after all.

25. We woke to a snowy Christmas morning; sunshine later and sharp frost at night.

26. Another heavy fall of snow in the night.

27. In the paper today it reports that all Britain lies under snow from John o'Groats to Land's End for the first time for six years.

> Amid the leafless thorn
>   the merry wren,
> When icicles hang dripping
>   from the rock,
> Pipes her perennial lay;
> Even when the flakes
> Broad on her pinions fall,
> She lightly flies
> Athwart the shower
>   and sings upon the wing.

James Graham.

Christmases at
Coughton Court

CHARLES LINES

Traditional Christmas parties in the great stately homes of
Warwickshire are now few and far between, but recollec-
tions of family celebrations at Coughton Court near
Alcester at the beginning of the century provide a taste of
their splendour. Charles Lines, who lives in Leamington
Spa, has written many authoritative works on the history
of English country houses and their families.

Christmas trees loaded with presents for indoor and outdoor
staff; servants' parties on a big scale; special plum-puddings,
ceremonially mixed; gifts for the aged poor; fires reflected in
ancient panelling; perhaps a visit from the mummers. The
old-time country-house Christmas party seems to belong to a
remote and feudal age. Yet such festivities were once common
in the great Midland mansions where 'good old families' are
recalled almost nostalgically by elderly countryfolk. One such
party was held for years earlier this century at Coughton Court
near Alcester, family home of the Throckmortons and now a
National Trust possession.

Elaborate and careful preparations were made. The Christmas pudding had stout in it and the mixing was an important
event in itself. It was enjoyed by the old people in Coughton

village, and poultry was also sent to them. On Christmas Eve, apart from the holly and other decorations, a tree about fourteen feet high was brought into the big Saloon with its branching staircase.

A ritual followed. The oranges – a greater 'treat' then than now – were always tied on first; the many candles came last. The selection of presents was an anxious matter. The Coughton housekeeper did her best to find out what each recipient would like. One year, I am told, the younger members of the household staff all had hot water-bottles, which sound a bit dull, but Coughton Court is not the warmest of houses.

As well as the oranges, the estate children had sweets and toys, the presents being handed to them by Coughton's chatelaine, Mrs Lilian Throckmorton, later Lilian, Lady Throckmorton of beloved memory. Including the children and the fourteen indoor staff, there would be some sixty to eighty at the party.

There was a high tea in the Servants' Hall where today's visitors to the Court now have their tea on opening days. This was in the late afternoon – a good spread of things like cold meats, jellies and mince-pies. The latter were always hot, although brought, like all food for the Servants' Hall, across the open courtyard. As this repast followed the staff Christmas dinner, it is evident that some folk were in no danger of starving!

The Throckmortons themselves had a house party for family and relatives, while various neighbours came in on Christmas Day. The gentry dined upstairs in the magnificent wainscoted dining-room.

Then there were charades with elaborate costumes. One year, Leonard Parkes, the village postmaster – a well-remembered local figure renowned for his appearances in light opera – took the part of Henry VIII. Sir Robert Throckmorton

· A Warwickshire Christmas ·

Leonard Parkes, Coughton's postmaster, as Henry VIII
(seated) with members of the Throckmorton family, in one
of the Coughton Court pantomimes

was one of the unfortunate wives, and his uncle, Mr Geoffrey
Throckmorton, another. On a different occasion, the theme
was that of pirates, with Mr Parkes appearing as a fairy with a
yellow wig and a tulle skirt. The framework of the boat was
made by estate staff.

Started early in the century, these magnificent parties
continued through the first world war, though in 1916, the
future Sir Robert's father, then heir to the baronetcy, was
killed in Mesopotamia – on the same day, incidentally, that
the family coat-of-arms fell from the Tudor gatehouse.

Although not always resident at Coughton, the Throckmortons have been closely connected with this spot since 1409,
when Sir John Throckmorton, Under-Treasurer of England,

33

married the Spiney heiress. The house, which has seen gay and grave times, is a fascinating mixture of styles and periods, with that fine gatehouse as its prominent feature.

Once moated, the old and romantic mansion contains many notable family portraits, tapestries, Jacobite relics and furniture. It also has a remarkable collection of family documents. A search among them might reveal details of earlier Christmases; one wonders if Bessie Throckmorton, who secretly married Sir Walter Raleigh, ever enjoyed Christmas at Coughton. Be that as it may, the parties I have briefly recalled show the happy family spirit which could prevail on a great estate.

Epitaph to a Countess

The splendid Beauchamp Chapel in the Collegiate Church of St Mary at Warwick, with its wealth of monuments and effigies reflecting momentous chapters in English history, contains a remarkable epitaph to Lettice, Countess of Leicester, third wife of Robert Dudley, Earl of Leicester, favourite of Elizabeth I. The Countess died 'upon Christmas Day in the morning' in 1634.

Looke in this vault and search it well
Much treasure in it lately fell
Wee all are robd and all doe say
Our wealth was carried this away
And that the theft might nere be found
Tis buried closely under ground
Yet if you gently stirr the mould
There all our losse you may behould
There may you see that face that hand
Which once was fairest in the land
She that in her younger yeares
Matcht with two great English peares
She that did supply the warrs
With thunder and the court with stars
She that in her youth had bene
Darling to the Maiden Queene
Till she was content to quitt
Her favoure for her Favoritt
Whose gould threed when she saw spunn
And the death of her brave sonn
Thought it safest to retyre
From all care and vaine desire
To a private countrie cell
Where she spent her dayes soe well
That to her the better sort
Came as to an holy court
And the poore that lived neare
Dearth nor Famine could not feare
Whilst she liv'd she lived thus
Till that God displeas'd with us
Suffred her at last to fall
Not from Him but from us all
And because she tooke delight
Christ's poore members to invite

He fully now requites her love
And sends His Angels from above
That did to Heaven her Soule convay
To solemnize His owne birth day

Christmas Was Such Fun

URSULA BLOOM

*The second selection of Christmas reminiscences from
Ursula Bloom again takes us back to the early years of the
century, when life in the remote villages of south Warwickshire still had a feudal ring about it, and the festive
season was a time of true magic, even for the daughter of
the rector.*

Christmas at the start of the century was such fun. In those days
children were children, and grown-ups were grown-ups, and it
was pretty well impossible to get into a grown-up party if you
came into that dreaded category known as being 'too young'!
I particularly remember Christmas at Warwick Castle. If ever

you want the most wonderful toy in all the world, let me tell you that it's a portcullis. Wonderful, that is, until you get too familiar with the way it works, and let it down on the wrong person. Our wrong person was a visiting bishop, who was – quite understandably I suppose – most unpleasant about it.

One of my friends was a boy called Maynard Greville. He was around my age, and his mother was the famous Lady Warwick who had that gift of beauty which made you think that the sunshine had come into the room as soon as she entered! She was, however, an extravagant lady, wildly generous, and she bought anything that she fancied. I remember the Christmas tree in the yellow drawing-room (that was the era of different coloured drawing-rooms; today only palaces have them). I was given a fairy doll, which, at Christmas, is a little girl's dream. My brother got a sailing yacht. Maynard had a humming top, but he took an instant dislike to it because it only played Christmas carols. I remember he had a row with his nanny, which shocked me. It was quite unprecedented to argue with one's nanny.

Next morning, a man came round to the castle selling – of all things – baby elephants. It sounds incredible, but at the start of the century anything could happen. Dancing bears frequently visited country houses, and there were hurdy-gurdies with budgerigars on top which told your fortune. I must admit there was a certain sameness about the fortunes, for the lady would always marry a rich and handsome stranger, and a gentleman would wed a lady as beautiful as the morning! Like that, all were satisfied.

The mahout who appeared with these particular baby elephants, knew that Lady Warwick could never say no. She bought one. 'It's such a dear little thing to have round the place,' said she. I remember my father choking slightly, and then saying: 'But what on earth will you do when it grows up?'

It stayed there quite a time and I saw it often. If you

annoyed it, it just picked you up and put you down on the other side of the hedge. In the end it was given to a zoo where it took children for rides at a handsome profit. 'I wish we'd thought of that for Warwick,' said her ladyship, a trifle sadly.

Christmas with Marie Corelli was not so much fun, but she did have wonderful crackers. In those days they had much livelier crackers than we do now. I remember that Marie Corelli always had to be the star turn and she would often play the harp to us. She invited the choir in to sing to us during Christmas evening, and on the previous afternoon all of us tied up five-bob bits into paper bags, to give to each of the choirboys.

There were Christmas concerts everywhere, and carol parties. There were also the hand-bell ringers who had parties of their own. Privately, each village competed, one with another, for the best set of carol singers. These singers would walk miles, often in dreadfully bad weather, and the owners of the big houses gave them pies and plum puddings, or 'something in the box'. There were the yellow oranges too, and, of course, the good wishes. Sometimes there was wine, if the master of the house was generous; cooking sherry if not.

Those were the days when presents came from everywhere. Even the grocer gave you a gift with the delivery of 'the Christmas order'. This was nearly always an almanac in gaudy colours, which graced the kitchen for the next year. He also sent me some chocolate biscuits which were very welcome. The patron of the living – we lived in Whitchurch rectory and my father was rector – sent round game galore. Much of it had to go down the well in a bucket, to keep it cool and edible until we were ready to eat it. The editor of the local newspaper gave a turkey for a year's contributions from my father, and I would have said that we did fairly well.

But what a disappointment it was that, having only one bell in our church, we could never give Christmas what we thought

Ursula Bloom and her brother Joscelyn in the garden of
Whitchurch Rectory at the beginning of the century

was due credit. Lower Quinton church rang hymn tunes most
beautifully. Ilmington managed a 'Grandsire Double', but
they had once had Simon de Montfort as their patron and they
felt that something was expected of them!

One day, my father took me and one of my friends –
Richard Aldington, who was a little older than me – up the
tower to see the Ilmington bells. They terrified me. The first
treble bore the inscription: *Soli Deo, Soli Gloria*. It had the

arms of King Charles I round the waist, and the motto *Honi soit qui mal y pense.*

Richard Aldington was at Dover College at that time, and, I presumed, quite learned. I did not know what *Honi soit* meant, and dared not appeal to the grown-ups, for sometimes that caused a row. In a whisper, I asked him: 'Do tell me what it means.' I don't really think that he knew any better than I did, for he whispered back a completely unlikely answer. Mercifully I never quoted him.

The coming of the New Year was never such a thrill as Christmas. By then we were too party-conscious, I suppose. The new century came when I was very small. 'You have got to remember this,' my father said, 'and so that you can remember it, you will be woken up and brought down to see the new century come in.'

It sounded exciting.

I was awakened, warned not to cry, and taken to see the beginning of the century. Believe me, the valley looked exactly the same as it had always done. Nothing happened. Bells did peal, it was true, but as we had only the one bell we could not compete, and it was not very interesting.

Christmas, though, is a wonderful time. It asserts itself. It dresses up in tinsel and glitter; it brings gifts and cards and a certain thrill which even now gets me every time. It is that lovely break in the dark heart of winter, and even if all the worst weather still lies beyond it, we don't think of it at Christmas time. Perhaps its joy lies in the fact that it is entirely different from any other time of the year, and we ourselves become entirely different to meet it.

from

Silas Marner

GEORGE ELIOT

Mary Ann Evans was born in Nuneaton in 1819. She is, of course, better known as George Eliot, the pseudonym under which she wrote, to gain acceptance in a world where women writers were generally taken less than seriously. Many of her novels were based on places and people – often thinly disguised – in her native county, and in Silas Marner *the village of Raveloe could well have been any Warwickshire village. In this extract, Silas the weaver, having suffered the ignominy of a robbery in which he lost his savings, works alone in his cottage at Christmastime, morose and introspective. In a bid to cheer him up, and urge him to celebrate Christmas by going to church, the well-meaning village woman Dolly Winthrop calls on Silas with her son Aaron, 'an apple-cheeked youngster of seven, with a clean starched frill'.*

'Dear heart!' said Dolly, pausing before she spoke again. 'But what a pity it is you should work of a Sunday, and not clean yourself – if you *didn't* go to church; for if you'd a roasting bit, it might be as you couldn't leave it, being a lone man. But there's the bakehus, if you could make up your mind to spend a twopence on the oven now and then – not every week, in

41

course – I shouldn't like to do that myself – you might carry your bit o' dinner there, for it's nothing but right to have a bit o' summat hot of a Sunday, and not to make it as you can't know your dinner from Saturday. But now, upon Christmas day, this blessed Christmas as is ever coming, if you was to take your dinner to the bakehus, and go to church, and see the holly and yew, and hear the anthim, and then take the sacramen', you'd be a deal the better, and you'd know which end you stood on, and you could put your trust i' Them as knows better nor we do, seein' you'd ha' done what it lies on us all to do.'

Dolly's exhortation, which was an unusually long effort of speech for her, was uttered in the soothing persuasive tone with which she would have tried to prevail on a sick man to take his medicine, or a basin of gruel for which he had no appetite. Silas had never before been closely urged on the point of his absence from church, which had only been thought of as a part of his general queerness; and he was too direct and simple to evade Dolly's appeal.

'Nay, nay,' he said, 'I know nothing o' church. I've never been to church.'

'No!' said Dolly, in a low tone of wonderment. Then bethinking herself of Silas's advent from an unknown country, she said, 'Could it ha' been as they'd no church where you was born?'

'O yes,' said Silas, meditatively, sitting in his usual posture of leaning on his knees, and supporting his head. 'There was churches – a many – it was a big town. But I knew nothing of 'em – I went to chapel.'

Dolly was much puzzled at this new word, but she was rather afraid of inquiring further, lest 'chapel' meant some haunt of wickedness. After a little thought, she said –

'Well, Master Marner, it's niver too late to turn over a new leaf, and if you've niver had no church, there's no telling the

good it'll do you. For I feel so set up and comfortable as niver was, when I've been and heard the prayers, and the singing to the praise and glory o' God . . . and if a bit o' trouble comes, I feel as I can put up wi' it, for I've looked for help i' the right quarter, and gev myself up to Them as we must all give ourselves up to at the last; and if we'n done our part, it isn't to be believed as Them as are above us 'ull be worse nor we are, and come short o' Their'n.'

Poor Dolly's exposition of her simple Raveloe theology fell rather unmeaningly on Silas's ears, for there was no word in it that could rouse a memory of what he had known as religion, and his comprehension was quite baffled by the plural pronoun, which was no heresy of Dolly's, but only her way of avoiding a presumptuous familiarity. He remained silent, not feeling inclined to assent to the part of Dolly's speech which he fully understood – her recommendation that he should go to church. Indeed, Silas was so unaccustomed to talk beyond the brief questions and answers necessary for the transaction of his simple business, that words did not easily come to him without the urgency of a distinct purpose.

But now, little Aaron, having become used to the weaver's awful presence, had advanced to his mother's side, and Silas, seeming to notice him for the first time, tried to return Dolly's signs of goodwill by offering the lad a bit of lard-cake. Aaron shrank back a little, and rubbed his head against his mother's shoulder, but still thought the piece of cake worth the risk of putting his hand out for it.

'O, for shame, Aaron,' said his mother, taking him on her lap, however; 'why, you don't want cake again yet awhile.'

She stroked Aaron's brown head, and thought it must do Master Marner good to see such a 'picture of a child'. But Marner, on the other side of the hearth, saw the neat-featured rosy face as a mere dim round, with two dark spots in it.

'And he's got a voice like a bird – you wouldn't think,'

· *A Warwickshire Christmas* ·

Dolly went on; 'he can sing a Christmas carril as his father's taught him; and I take it for a token as he'll come to good, as he can learn the good tunes so quick. Come, Aaron, stan' up and sing the carril to Master Marner, come.'

Aaron replied by rubbing his forehead against his mother's shoulder.

'O, that's naughty,' said Dolly, gently. 'Stan' up, when mother tells you, and let me hold the cake till you've done.'

Aaron was not indisposed to display his talents, even to an ogre, under protecting circumstances; and after a few more signs of coyness, consisting chiefly in rubbing the backs of his hands over his eyes, and then peeping between them at Master Marner, to see if he looked anxious for the 'carril', he at length allowed his head to be duly adjusted, and standing behind the table, which let him appear above it only as far as his broad frill, so that he looked like a cherubic head untroubled with a body, he began with a clear chirp, and in a melody that had the rhythm of an industrious hammer –

> God rest you merry, gentlemen,
> Let nothing you dismay,
> For Jesus Christ our Saviour
> Was born on Christmas day.

Dolly listened with a devout look, glancing at Marner in some confidence that this strain would help to allure him to church.

'That's Christmas music,' she said, when Aaron had ended, and had secured his piece of cake again. 'There's no other music equil to the Christmas music – "Hark the erol angils sing". And you may judge what it is at church Master Marner . . .'

The Christmas carol, with its hammer-like rhythm, had fallen on his ears as strange music, quite unlike a hymn, and could have none of the effect Dolly contemplated. But he

44

wanted to show her that he was grateful and the only mode that occurred to him was to offer Aaron a bit more cake.

'O, no, thank you, Master Marner,' said Dolly, holding down Aaron's willing hands. 'We must be going home now.'

Silas said, 'Good-bye, and thank you kindly', as he opened the door for Dolly, but he couldn't help feeling relieved when she was gone – relieved that he might weave again and moan at his ease. Her simple view of life and its comforts, by which she had tried to cheer him, was only like a report of unknown objects, which his imagination could not fashion.

And so, Silas spent his Christmas Day in loneliness, eating his meat in sadness of heart, though the meat had come to him as a neighbourly present. In the morning he looked out on the black frost that seemed to press cruelly on every blade of grass, while the half-icy red pool shivered under the bitter wind; but towards evening the snow began to fall, and curtained from him even that dreary outlook, shutting him close up with his narrow grief. And he sat in his robbed home through the livelong evening, not caring to close his shutters or lock his door, pressing his head between his hands and moaning, till the cold grasped him and told him that his fire was grey.

Nobody in this world but himself knew that he was the same Silas Marner who had once loved his fellow with tender love, and trusted in an unseen goodness. Even to himself that past experience had become dim.

But in Raveloe village the bells rang merrily, and the church was fuller than all through the rest of the year, with red faces among the abundant dark-green boughs – faces prepared for a longer service than usual by an odorous breakfast of toast and ale.

Those green boughs, the hymn and anthem never heard but at Christmas – even the Athanasian Creed, which was discriminated from the others only as being longer and of exceptional virtue, since it was only read on rare occasions –

brought a vague exulting sense, for which the grown men could as little have found words as the children, that something great and mysterious had been done for them in heaven above, and in earth below, which they were appropriating by their presence. And then the red faces made their way through the black biting frost to their own homes, feeling themselves free for the rest of the day to eat, drink, and be merry, and using that Christian freedom without diffidence.

from

Daisy Daisy

DAISY ENGLAND

Daisy England's poignant account of her working-class childhood in the years immediately following the First World War reveals almost unbelievable contrasts with a child's life today. Moving with her family from London to a Midland village in 1918, she found that happiness was so often a transient luxury to be cherished, and that unhappiness was never far below the surface. Yet she somehow coped with the trauma of her father leaving home, with incarceration in a workhouse with her younger sister, and with the ever-present spectre of poverty. Christmastime

· *A Warwickshire Christmas* ·

*was hardly less dreary than any other time of the year.
In this first extract, Daisy recalls her first post-war
Christmas after leaving London, and a shopping expedi-
tion laced with disappointment.*

Christmas with church bells, carols and roast beef; an apple, an
orange and a pink sugar mouse made limp stuffing for each of
the three black stockings hung with happy expectation at the
bed rail. Handkerchiefs and hair ribbons arrived by post from
the good aunt and cousins. A working-class Christmas at that
time lacked the extravaganza we know today. The traditional
turkey and glittering Christmas tree belonged essentially to
the middle classes and the landed gentry, a gulf accepted, and
just then in the shared relief of a new-found peace on earth, it
hardly mattered.

Prior to the festive season we had walked the long distance
to the little town beyond the park via the grandparents, not for
Christmas provisions but a new coat for the elder sister. A
suitable one was found, and for good measure, a hat too of such
jaunty chic as to be remembered for ever: a four-sectioned
black velvet artist's beret with long silken cord and tassel of
the same swinging buoyancy as found on a pull-down blind.

With open purse and the bobbing darling at the spender's
elbow, the spree ended with gloves to complete the outfit. In
youthful pique at this avalanche of priority I ventured the
gloves should rightly be for one of us others, as our coats were
without pockets, and the new garment had deep ones, a
coveted touch of style and a real comfort for cold hands. This
cry from the wilderness was hardly heard as the new ensemble
was packed for carrying home.

In the centre of the town a large house was being used as a
convalescent home for wounded soldiers. We saw many of
these men that day, their martial invalidism symbolized by the
familiar sugar-bag blue; one-armed, one-legged, on crutches

and in bath chairs, paying the greatest price for freedom this side of the grave.

> *The following Christmas was a similarly lack-lustre affair, culminating in a bitter feud between her parents, and her father's aggressive departure from the family home.*

Christmas again. Joylessly we harkened to the herald angels, and our stockings hung limp and empty. School holidays were prolonged for reasons long since forgotten. With this grace we aimlessly meandered the wintry lanes with the other young of the village. We loitered too at farmyard gates on those days when the threshing machine chugged its background monotone to the demoniacal cries of men armed with sticks, and the yelps of frenzied dogs encircling the cornstack as it was slowly unwalled to feed into the machine, disrupting hundreds of rats and mice, checked in flight by victorious clubbers and canine jaws.

The dreary winter wore on. The school re-opened, and education was resumed. One day we returned home to enter an arena of battle the like of which hitherto was unknown even to us. Clearly amnesty could play no part in the ceasefire. As the tumult died, the aggressor flung himself from us, and we sat stunned in wretched silence, awaiting his invigorated return. But he didn't come, not that night nor the next day nor the next.

> *Christmas the next year found Daisy and her younger sister approaching the end of their term in the workhouse where the festive season at least received minimal acknowledgement. Ahead lay the fresh challenges of 'adoption' by a sympathetic local family, of leaving school at fourteen, and of the privations of life in domestic service.*

Christmas came, and Christmas passed, with memory's holly-boughs decorating the window ledges of the dining-hall, festive setting for the concessionary luxury of Christmas pudding and beer. Even for those of such mean expectancy there was a tea party, followed by a concert given by a local organization. It was whilst in the cosy coma of youthful contentment and the lowered lights of the improvised 'house' (dining-hall), I first ever smelt the fragrance of percolating coffee. Later that evening, from a cup complete with saucer, I discovered how phenomenal promise surpassed fulfilment, the same vague disappointment that allegedly surrounds the breakfast rasher.

Meanwhile, before a cheerful fire at the cosiest end of the boardroom, with sewing machine, lengths of material and our own not too consuming measurements, a daily dressmaker worked to prepare our trousseau for the outside world.

Daisy England survived it all. She later married, had two daughters and a son, and now lives in happy retirement in the Warwickshire village of Wellesbourne.

Christmas Eve

WASHINGTON IRVING

*The American essayist Washington Irving wrote exten-
sively about his travels in England in the early years of the
last century. One of his best-known works is* Bracebridge
Hall, *widely assumed to have been based on Aston Hall,
the fine Jacobean mansion in Birmingham. This book was
a sequel to the essays portraying Christmas at Bracebridge
Hall which had appeared earlier as an anonymous
collection entitled* The Sketch Book of Geoffrey
Crayon, Gent. *This first extract from the Sketch Book
comes from the Christmas Eve essay, which recounts a
visit to the Hall in the company of Squire Bracebridge's
son Frank.*

As we approached the house, we heard the sound of music, and
now and then a burst of laughter, from one end of the
building. This, Bracebridge said, must proceed from the
servants' hall, where a great deal of revelry was permitted, and
even encouraged, by the squire, throughout the twelve days of
Christmas, provided everything was done conformably to
ancient usage.

Here were kept up the old games of hoodman blind, shoe
the wild mare, hot cockles, steal the white loaf, bob apple, and
snap dragon. The yule log and Christmas candle were regularly
burnt, and the mistletoe, with its white berries, hung up, to
the imminent peril of all the pretty housemaids.

· A Warwickshire Christmas ·

'The waits went round the house, playing under the windows'

So intent were the servants upon their sports, that we had to ring repeatedly before we could make ourselves heard. On our arrival being announced, the squire came out to receive us accompanied by his two other sons; one a young officer in the army, home on leave of absence; the other an Oxonian, just from the university.

The squire was a fine healthy-looking old gentleman, with silver hair curling lightly round an open florid countenance; in which the physiognomist, with the advantage, like myself, of a previous hint or two, might discover a singular mixture of whim and benevolence.

The family meeting was warm and affectionate. As the evening was far advanced, the squire would not permit us to change our travelling dresses, but ushered us at once to the company, which was assembled in a large old-fashioned hall.

The grate had been removed from the wide overwhelming fireplace, to make way for a fire of wood, in the midst of which

was an enormous log glowing and blazing, and sending forth a vast volume of light and heat; this I understood was the yule log, which the squire was particular in having brought in and illumined on Christmas Eve, according to ancient custom. Herrick mentions it in one of his songs –

> Come, bring with a noise,
> My merrie, merrie boyes,
> The Christmas log to the firing;
> While my good dame, she
> Bids ye all be free,
> And drink to your heart's desiring.

Supper was announced shortly after our arrival. It was served up in a spacious oaken chamber, the panels of which shone with wax, and around which were several family portraits decorated with holly and ivy. Besides the accustomed lights, two great wax tapers, called Christmas candles, wreathed with greens, were placed on a highly-polished beaufet among the family plate. The table was abundantly spread with substantial fare; but the squire made his supper of frumenty, a dish made of wheat cakes boiled in milk, with rich spices, being a standing dish in old times for Christmas Eve. I was happy to find my old friend, minced pie, in the retinue of the feast; and finding him to be perfectly orthodox, and that I need not be ashamed of my predilection, I greeted him with all the warmth wherewith we usually greet an old and very genteel acquaintance.

The supper had disposed every one to gaiety, and an old harper was summoned from the servants' hall, where he had been strumming all evening, and to all appearance comforting himself with some of the squire's home-brewed. The dance, like most dances after supper, was a merry one; some of the older folks joined in it. . . .

· A Warwickshire Christmas ·

The yule log is dragged into the house

The party now broke up for the night with the kind-hearted old custom of shaking hands. As I passed the hall, on my way to my chamber, the dying embers of the yule log still sent forth a dusky glow, and had it not been the season when 'no spirit dares stir abroad', I should have been half tempted to steal from my room at midnight, and peep whether the fairies might not be at their revels about the hearth.

My chamber was in the old part of the mansion, the ponderous furniture of which might have been fabricated in the days of the giants. The room was panelled, with cornices of heavy carved work, in which flowers and grotesque faces were strangely intermingled; and a row of black-looking portraits stared mournfully at me from the walls. The bed was of rich though faded damask, with a lofty tester, and stood in a niche opposite a bow window.

I had scarcely got into bed when a strain of music seemed to break forth in the air just below the window. I listened, and found it proceeded from a band, which I concluded to be the waits from some neighbouring village. They went round the house, playing under the windows. I drew aside the curtains to hear them more distinctly. The moonbeams fell through the upper part of the casement, partially lighting up the antiquated apartment. The sounds, as they receded, became more soft and aerial, and seemed to accord with the quiet and moonlight. I listened and listened – they became more and more tender and remote, and, as they gradually died away, my head sunk upon the pillow, and I fell asleep.

Grimaldi's Last Birmingham Pantomime

GILBERT MOORE

Joseph Grimaldi, one of the greatest pantomime performers of all time, was at the height of his career in the early years of the last century despite a latent illness from which

54

· A Warwickshire Christmas ·

he died in 1837. His last Christmas pantomime in Birmingham, as writer and journalist Gilbert Moore relates here, was evidently a remarkable success.

Celebrated, Grimaldi certainly was: as a clown in pantomime he was without equal. Birmingham still talked about his previous visit in 1808 when, finding no property fowl for his act, he sent to the Bull Ring Market for some live ones. Joe, as the traditional comic servant in spotted pantaloons and cap and bells, eventually came on stage with a duck's head peeping out of each capacious pocket, a live goose under one arm and a piglet under the other, extemporizing brilliantly with his lively stooges.

Now, Birmingham was to see him in his prime, at forty-two, in a Christmas pantomime which had run at Covent Garden for fifty-seven nights. As was customary in those days, London pantomimes afterwards went on tour, so that the provinces enjoyed one of their Christmas festivities in mid-summer. *Harlequin and Friar Bacon, or The Brazen Head*, was one of the new *speaking* pantomimes, which had been in vogue since the introduction of dialogue at Sadler's Wells a year or two before. Pantos were no longer purely mime, but Joseph Grimaldi, who had been on the boards since the age of three, had negotiated the barrier between silence and speech as dexterously as one of his own gambols.

Harlequin and Friar Bacon, or The Brazen Head was the most ambitious pantomime the Royal had ever staged. 'The tricks and machinery,' announced the management proudly, 'are *actually* those used at Covent Garden; the scenery has been painted by the same artists.' The pantomime was produced and supervised by Grimaldi himself.

It was one of the last true pantomimes, featuring Harlequin and Columbine, Grimaldi's servant-clown, and two incidental characters, one of which was played by Grimaldi's nineteen-

55

year-old son, an ill-disciplined lad, whose short-lived career was to end in a drunken delirium.

The pantomime was an enormous success, despite the counter-attraction of the Coronation of His Majesty, King George IV, four days before, and the town's illuminations and festivities. Grimaldi's inimitable grimaces, his trips and gambols, his rendering of the popular ditties 'Tippety Witchet' and 'Hot Codlins', were greeted with the wildest enthusiasm, and he left the stage at the end of each scene to an avalanche of laughter and applause.

But in the wings, a terrible transformation scene took place. From an apparently agile young man, Grimaldi would suddenly slump to decrepitude, gripped by a premature ageing which had been coming upon him for some months, completely baffling his physicians. Only by a great effort of will was he able, while on stage, to resist it; but the moment he reached the wings, his limbs shook violently, and he was quite unable to support himself. He was carried to his dressing room, where he was feverishly massaged, to prepare him for the next scene.

Out of sight of his mirth-shaking audience, Grimaldi went through this ghastly charade after each scene of every performance, wearing simultaneously the masks of tragedy and comedy. It seemed as if Life, resentful at his making so much fun of it, was determined upon revenge.

Yet each of his twenty-four performances was uniformly brilliant. As far as his audience was concerned, packing the theatre from its apple-green and crimson boxes to its crystal chandeliers, there was no apparent reason why Grimaldi should not be Grimaldi. When not actually at the theatre, he was reasonably recovered, and made the most of his Birmingham stay by having his portrait painted. It was carried out by a Mr S. Raven, on a large circular papier mâché box, and the resemblance was so pleasing that Joseph had half a dozen made, to distribute among his friends.

For his services, the Royal Theatre's manager, Mr Bunn, paid him handsomely, with a salary of £20 per week for Joe himself and £9 for his son. Joseph Grimaldi often spoke of Mr Bunn's liberality, and when Bunn went to London to manage a theatre there, but for some reason fell into disfavour, he found Joseph a firm ally.

Harlequin and Friar Bacon was the last pantomime the great Grimaldi played in Birmingham, though he did visit the Royal again twelve months later when, having met Mr Bunn at Cheltenham, where Grimaldi was taking a rest cure, the great clown was persuaded to play in a sketch of his own devising called *Puck and the Puddings*.

This sketch was Joseph Grimaldi's last professional appearance of all. His health so deteriorated that, after a farewell performance at Covent Garden in 1828, the most famous of all English clowns took off the motley for good, and nine years later passed away.

Festive Fare of Yesteryear

CHARLES LINES

Old recipes for dishes intended for the Christmas season have a strange fascination, especially when compared with

*the pre-packed ingredients available in our modern age of
the freezer and microwave. Charles Lines's intimate
knowledge of the historic country houses of Warwickshire
gave him in 1981 a rare opportunity to reveal some of the
seasonal secrets of the great kitchens in an age long gone.*

Partly inspired by recipes for Frances, Countess of Warwick's
sherry cakes and an unusual Christmas pudding, I began
asking those living in Warwickshire country-houses for their
own recipes, old and new – but I scarcely anticipated the
generous response.

Ragley, Coughton, Charlecote, Newnham Paddox and
many other historic homes have yielded a positive flood of
fascinating 'receipts', which often make my mouth water, but
just occasionally cause a shudder!

Betty, Countess of Denbigh (the Feildings, Earls of
Denbigh, have owned the Newnham Paddox estate, near
Rugby, for centuries) has given me a recipe for 'An old
partridge to be eaten cold'. You prepare the bird for cooking,
wrap it entirely in bacon, tying it on if necessary. Put the
partridge in cold salt water and bring to the boil. Leave it to
simmer for forty minutes, or until tender, testing with a fork.
Leave in the water till cold. Unwrap the bacon and serve on a
dish decorated with parsley or a little lettuce.

Lady Denbigh says that 'this used to be a favourite breakfast
dish, as the partridge is full of flavour and tender, but is now
usually eaten as a main course, with salad or jacket potato'.

Another partridge recipe comes from Sir William Dugdale
of Blyth Hall, Coleshill. It is, alas, too long and complicated
for me to give it in full, and you would certainly need a
kitchenmaid or two to 'cut about a hundred pieces of carrot,
half an inch in length', and peel sixty small button onions,
amid a host of other tasks.

Sir William, however, also gives me 'Mutton Pique', taken

from Ann Stratford's housebook of around 1735. (The Stratfords of Merevale Hall, Atherstone, were Dugdale ancestors). It consists simply of the 'thick part of neck of mutton without fat, all the bottom part of the bones taken off, larded through, seared with fire top and bottom, stewed with wood ashes very slow'.

It reminds me that boiled mutton was almost invariably served at the so-called 'Ice-Supper' enjoyed into the present century at Elmdon Hall, near Solihull, by all the estate workers who had helped to fill the huge ice-house in the grounds.

Warwickshire has long been celebrated for its deer-parks, now sadly reduced in number, and my own father used to recall that venison was hung in the trees at Packington Park near Meriden, until it was well and 'high'.

'As far as the cooking of deer is concerned,' says Alice, Lady Fairfax-Lucy of Charlecote, 'the dear old cook, when I married, used a method as old as Shakespeare. She cooked it in what she called a "pastry overcoat", very slowly for a long time.'

The Packington venison would certainly not be to my taste, and I am a little concerned about the 'pig disguised' which figured at a dinner party given by Mistress Jane Holbech at Bentley Heath manor house in 1728, together with 'peachick, whole preserved lemons and snow', as one guest, Dr Andrew Archer, Rector of Solihull, expired soon afterwards.

After this, I think that 'Rice Cream – Arbury, 1843' from Mr Francis FitzRoy Newdegate, whose family seat, near Nuneaton, is perhaps the best 'Gothick' house in the country, would be quite welcome.

'Wash and pick some rice, boil till quite soft, drain it on a sieve till nearly dry. Line a pudding dish with the rice (not pressing it too hard), whisk a pint of cream till very stiff, add sugar which has been rubbed on lemon peel, and the juice of two lemons, and 1 oz of clarified isinglass (cold). Pour it into

Bringing in the Christmas dinner

the rice, and when firm spread orange marmalade over it.
When wanted, turn it out on to the dish you intend to serve at
table.'

I would certainly like to try 'Sir William Throckmorton's
Brown Plum Cake', which was once served at his home,
Coughton Court near Alcester. It needs 1 lb flour, $\frac{1}{2}$ lb of butter,
1 lb of stoned raisins, $\frac{1}{2}$ lb of brown sugar, $1\frac{1}{2}$ teaspoonsful of
bicarbonate of soda, 2 eggs, mixed with a little less than half a
pint of milk. It has to be baked for five hours.

You might also care to try the sort of almond cakes once
eaten at Coughton by the Throckmorton household and
described in an early manuscript 'receipt' book. You will need

'a pound of almonds and a pound of fine sugar, 5 whites of eggs and 2 yolks; beate them very well and strain them in 8 spoonfulls of rose water and 5 or 6 spoonfulls of fine flower (*sic*). Blanch ye almonds and slice them with a knife, so mingle all these together and bake them in a silver plate'.

You would also require sweet almonds for a blancmange which, of course, did not come out of a packet from the supermarket in those days. Other ingredients were 'a pint of very stiff jelly of hartshorne' (shredded horn from hart or stag), new milk, orange-flower water and loaf sugar. This concoction was served in glasses and 'a cupple of bitter almonds must be put in with ye sweet almonds'.

I doubt if anyone these days will have the inclination to 'pott an otter' for part of their Christmas fare (even if the law and the otter population allowed), but you could 'bake ducks in a pott' with a seasoning of mace, cloves, nutmeg and salt, a pint of claret, the same of vinegar, 'some onyons' and bay leaves. I must admit I would certainly prefer the duck to 'roast eel', but if you would like to try it you must 'slitt ye skinn off it a little way, then pull off ye skinn and leave ye head upon it'. You then boil the innards until the flesh 'comes from ye bone, then mince it with dates, oysters and sweet herbs', as well as a little lemon diced. The mixture is then put back into the skin which has been 'scoured very well with salt and washed clean', the whole ghastly thing then being roasted and basted with butter.

The Throckmorton cook and her assistants, or the stillroom maids, would doubtless have made 'gilley flower', raspberry, currant, cowslip or gooseberry wines well before the festive season, and possibly wormwood wine or even 'a viper wine Sir Robert Paston's way'. For this last evil-sounding beverage, a couple of vipers were beheaded and immersed in sack (a dry Spanish wine). This, one gathers from the book, is 'a very great cordiall and good against leprosy'.

61

On balance, I think I'd prefer 'the Famous Gripe Water' containing two quarts of brandy, 'a pound of best carraway comfitts' and twelve grains of 'scutcheneel' (cochineal) and which, when made, should 'stand in ye sun or chimney where it may be warme'. It must have been urgently required after that roast eel!

from

As You Like It

WILLIAM SHAKESPEARE

Not surprisingly, Shakespeare derived ready inspiration from the countryside of his native Warwickshire, and in As You Like It, *several scenes are set in the great Forest of Arden, remnants of which survive to this day. Here, in a bitter Warwickshire winter, the exiled Duke addresses Amiens and other attendant lords in a forest clearing.*

Now, my co-mates and brothers in exile,
Hath not old custom made this life more sweet
Than that of painted pomp? Are not these woods
More free from peril than the envious court?
Here feel we but the penalty of Adam –
The seasons' difference: as the icy fang

William Shakespeare, Warwickshire's best-known literary
genius

And churlish chiding of the winter's wind,
Which when it bites and blows upon my body,
Even till I shrink with cold, I smile and say,
This is no flattery: these are counsellors
That feelingly persuade me what I am.
Sweet are the uses of adversity;
Which, like the toad, ugly and venomous,
Wears yet a precious jewel in his head;
And this our life, exempt from public haunt,
Finds tongues in trees, books in the running brooks,
Sermons in stones, and good in everything.
I would not change it.

And later, still in the forest, Amiens sings this seasonal
song —

Blow, blow, thou winter wind
Thou art not so unkind
As man's ingratitude;
Thy tooth is not so keen,
Because thou art not seen,
Although thy breath be rude.

Heigh-ho! sing heigh-ho! unto the green holly:
Most friendship is feigning, most loving mere folly:

Then heigh-ho, the holly
This life is most jolly.

Freeze, freeze, thou bitter sky,
That dost not bite so nigh
As benefits forgot:
Though thou the waters warp,

Thy sting is not so sharp
As friend remember'd not.

Heigh-ho! sing heigh-ho! unto the green holly:
Most friendship is feigning, most loving mere folly:

Then heigh-ho, the holly
This life is most jolly.

Christmas in Edwardian Leamington

FRANCES O'SHAUGHNESSY

*Frances O'Shaughnessy, author, teacher and ardent
Leamingtonian, wrote extensively about the town and was
closely involved with the Leamington Literary Society. Her
memories went back to the early years of the century, and
these evocative recollections of her childhood Christmases,
written in the 1950s, paint a graphic picture of the simple
pleasures of the festive season before commercialism and the
'progress' of social attitudes changed it for ever.*

65

· A Warwickshire Christmas ·

Christmas in town is never, by most of us, thought to be as traditional and 'rooted' as Christmas in the country, and yet in Leamington nearly half a century ago, there was a Dickensian flavour that perhaps has gone now for all time.

Always a cheerful place for a child at any time of the year, Leamington scintillated at the festive season. The shops were bedecked with the almost forgotten lavishness of the days before world wars were thought of, and I never tired of 'going shopping' with any relative who would take my eager hand. Strange how I recall the Christmas shops as always lit up in the evening rather than in the daylight.

Mine was a busy family and I suppose did most of its shopping in the evening. Not so strange perhaps when I reflect that shops could and did remain open until 9 and even 10 p.m., and to be out after dark was a special Christmas treat. The shops literally overflowed with good things, and though electricity was in its infancy then, the shops were ablaze with great gas mantles spreading their white light in the larger Parade shops, and fascinating acetylene flares spluttering outside the poulterers where window-sills and signboards and door posts and nameplates were all hidden by hosts of geese and turkeys, chickens and ducks. In the quieter streets the warmer light of naked gas jets went unspied as a means of Christmas lighting, nor did the rosy apples and gleaming oranges look any less attractive in these flickering beams.

My childhood was spent in St Mary's district, so that I knew the lower town streets best. High Street had a lure of its own. There was a cheerful grocer's on the corner where those flat oblong biscuits covered with smooth coffee sugar icing, each with the white shape of an intriguing animal superimposed, could be bought. Almost next door was the Penny Bazaar kept by two old ladies who never minded how long you took to make up your mind. They sold the most delightful little sacks of coloured glass beads (hundreds of them) for a penny, and

· A Warwickshire Christmas ·

The colonnaded Royal Pump Room, and the parish church
of All Saints at Leamington Spa in the early years of the
century

had a large tray of dolls ranging from one inch china dolls at
eight a penny to the twopenny ones I loved with their delicate
little porcelain faces and little china hands and feet, whose
obliging sawdust-filled bodies could be pinned or stitched
according to whim. You could buy a row of soldiers for a
penny and an infinite variety of musical instruments for the
same price.

Close by was Mrs Farmer's, whose cake shop was a work of
art at Christmas. Mr Farmer made the best halfpenny
doughnuts and coconut macaroons in the lower town, and
when it came to Christmas cakes he was an artist of the first
rank. How he got them all into the window was never
discovered. I can still smell the lovely aromas that wafted over
the threshold as the little shop door bell tinkled overhead.
There were two intriguing pork shops on the other side of the

· A *Warwickshire Christmas* ·

Tempting rows of potential Christmas dinners decorate the
shop-front of Colebrook & Co in 1911

High Street, and each a lesson in design, colour and arrangement, the centrepiece being a glazed pig's head decorated with
pink and white icing and having an apple in its mouth.
Sausages of all kinds, red, black and white, radiated from it,
stupendous pies filled in the background and choice cuts of
pork and bacon made new motifs.

I preferred the window show to the inside of these shops,
however, for so many dead porkers hung awaiting dismem-
berment around the tiled walls inside that they scared me to
death. I once saw a four-man German band in High Street, the
rotund Teutons blowing away at 'Silent Night' with their
brass trumpets while the busy Christmas shoppers whirled
around them.

These were the days when a child's Christmas revolved around the Holy Child's birthday and was inseparable from all that meant. There was life and meaning and light that shone through everything. We sang 'Once in Royal David's City', in the large shining, rather garish church, decked out in its holly and flowers. We heard the calm gentle voice of the dear old vicar telling us the old, old story in his own inimitable way: it was all part of Christmastime and became traditional to us. I knew nothing then of the attractions of old architecture in ancient churches, of the dim ecclesiastical atmosphere created by priceless old stained glass. This obvious product of the Victorian Age welcomed its children, was bright and warm, and its vicar and parishioners enclosed us in their Master's warmth. What more could a child ask?

Christmas Day was a family affair, the bigger the better, a day of homely fun to which everyone contributed something. Mendelssohn's 'Songs Without Words' was invariably played by someone, 'Messiah' choruses sung by those who could sing, Gilbert and Sullivan, especially the current one being given that year by the Leamington Operatic, tackled by everyone. When a quiet spell was indicated, a kind, clever young uncle would bring out a white screen, and turn out the gas in a breathless hush – the Magic Lantern. Slides pushed in, a handle turned and there on the screen would actually be a boy and girl, skipping, and in colour too! And as if to confound us after that, the gas was lit again and he brought out another magic box, this time with an enormous ungainly-looking horn on top, and in a minute or two we would hear a man's singing voice and music coming thinly from this amazing thing with its revolving disc. The thrill of my first wireless set, the wonder of my first television experience, nothing newly invented has ever given me the same feeling as I had when I first heard that reedy old phonograph.

When we took our candlesticks and went to our bedrooms

where artificial light had not yet penetrated, there was no electric fire to greet us, nor even a rubber hot water bottle. But Grandpa, bless his heart, had warmed the beds with the copper warming pan filled with glowing embers from the kitchen fire, and Grandma had warmed our little insides with her homemade ginger wine. We lay cosily listening for a little while to the clop-clop of the horses' feet as they clattered by with people going to and from parties in carriage, hansom cab or humble four-wheeler, and to merry pedestrians laughing as they walked home, and then we would sleep. Another peaceful Christmas Day was over.

from

Lock Keeper's Daughter

PAT WARNER

Birmingham's canals — more numerous, we are told, than those of Venice — radiate in all directions from the city which, until 1974, was well and truly a part of Warwickshire. Although Pat Warner's delightful reminiscences of a childhood Christmas largely belong to

· A Warwickshire Christmas ·

the canal linking Birmingham and Worcester, they are evocative of the life of almost any Midland canal family in the years between the wars.

The winter of 1928, it just snowed and snowed. We didn't see the milkman or the postman for a number of weeks. Somehow, this seemed fairly normal in those days and we were always well prepared.

The snow would pile up along the towing path, two or three feet high – sometimes higher. And it was cold. So cold at night that it would freeze the contents of the chamber pot under the bed! I would keep warm with a hot brick wrapped in a piece of flannel. But what a pretty sight was all that snow. Clean, white snow, not dirty slushy stuff. The sun shining and long icicles hanging from the lock gates. If you looked across the reservoir from the back bedroom window, you might catch a glimpse of some wild creature which had dared venture out. You might even see a red squirrel, sitting in one of the trees, holding a hazel nut between his front paws.

I knew that if the weather didn't improve, we would be unable to visit my aunt and uncle for Christmas. They lived, I thought, on the other side of the world, but it was only Wolverhampton. All that long distance was a great adventure for me. It began with a two-mile walk to the bus stop. . . .

On reaching journey's end, the Wolverhampton snow was all wet and dirty, not like the nice clean snow I was used to.

Most of Christmas Eve was passed in taking trams to visit the shops. What a good thing I liked trams and buses, because not all the dolls and sweets in England would have persuaded me to get into a car. I was terrified of motor cars. The large stores in town stayed open until 8 o'clock at night and I would be able to buy all my Christmas presents with the 2s. 6d. (12½p) I had saved.

We would return to my aunt's house for supper and go to

· *A Warwickshire Christmas* ·

'Clean white snow, not dirty slushy stuff . . .'

the midnight service at the huge church in nearby Cannock. There would be a big choir, a lovely crib and (as I then described it) the man with the flat hat would swing the innocents around! The smell of incense would stay in my nostrils for days. After we left church, my aunt and uncle would curse and argue all the way home.

Here at my aunt's I would sleep in a folding chair. I lay awake for hours, waiting for Father Christmas to come down the chimney. Somehow, I always missed him. I had the same presents in my stocking each year: a large coloured play ball, a sugar pig, an orange and one bright new shining penny.

Christmas in Wolverhampton meant more to me than anything else in the world. For once, there would be water

from the tap by the sink; gas light in the kitchen to show me the way across the yard to the WC outside; a gas stove in the kitchen on which to boil the kettle . . . all this was achieved at the turn of a switch. The mantle in the light globe made a funny hissing sound, quite warm and homely.

There were always nice things to eat, with little luxuries like sago pudding. On Christmas morning it was cold boiled ham for breakfast. Uncle worked for the railway and was 'rich'. Afterwards, we dressed in our Sunday best to attend the Christmas morning service. But first, always on a Christmas morning, without fail, my aunt would scrub the back yard. Down she went on her hands and knees and scrubbed and scrubbed. Meanwhile, my 'rich' uncle became madder and madder, shouting and blaspheming and then hoping that the Good Lord would forgive him.

If we were lucky, we might get our Christmas dinner about 3 p.m. I just couldn't wait for dinner to be cleared away because I knew that afterwards the grown-ups would play cards, so they wouldn't need me around. That could only mean one thing:

'Put little Pat into the parlour. There's a nice fire. She can amuse herself.'

A lovely fire cast its shadows on the parlour ceiling. It was the only day of the year that this room was open to the public apart from weddings and funerals. The 'holy of holies' shone brighter than the Eastern Star!

Cards finished, my uncle could settle down for the great moment he had been waiting for: a sing-song round the piano. The walls would ring with the rendering of fine old Victorian carols. My favourite was 'The Mistletoe Bough' by Thomas Haynes Bayly:

> The mistletoe hung in the castle hall.
> The holly branch shone on the old oak wall.

The Baron's retainers were blithe and gay
While keeping their Christmas holiday.
The Baron beheld with a fatherly pride
His beautiful child, young Lovell's bride.
She, with her bright eyes, seemed to be
The star of that goodly company.
Oh, the mistletoe bough.
Oh, the mistletoe bough.

Uncle Dick was a good pianist and that never-to-be-forgotten carol made a perfect Christmas. We went home the day after Boxing Day.

I didn't have a Christmas tree, either at home or at my aunt's. A holly bush would be hung from a large hook in the ceiling at home, provided that the home-cured bacon had first been removed. This top, taken from a holly tree, was a pretty sight, a bow of tinsel, a pink sugar pig and a white sugar mouse being the only decorations. But it filled the house with the spirit and magic of Christmas. I knew that the little pig, with his friend the mouse, would afterwards be returned to their paper wrappings for next Christmas . . . and the next . . . and the next. Eventually, they were so old, worn and dusty they were almost beyond recognition. I never knew what happened to them.

There is nothing to compare with a childhood Christmas. The waking at some unearthly hour for that wonderful moment when you looked for the presents. They were always there. The great preparations beforehand like sitting up through the night to boil the Christmas puddings in the copper. Mince pies were the size of saucers, covered in caster sugar and often washed down with a glass of Father's homemade 'poison'. It was an adventure to go tramping though the snow to gather the holly, ivy and mistletoe from some secret place. The snow was as fine and white as the icing

on the cake. And you must never forget to make a wish whilst stirring the Christmas puddings.

Childhood Christmas treats left a great impression on my mind. The magic of hanging up a pillow-case, the feel of the sugar pig and the orange lying hidden in one corner and most of all that wonderful faith in Father Christmas.

Home from Wolverhampton, it was strange to lie in my own bed again and to listen to the weird sounds of the cut instead of the rattling trams going up the Cannock Road. Father, too, enjoyed these Christmas treats as much as I did. Before we went away he would read Dickens's *A Christmas Carol* to me, the story of Scrooge and the ghosts and the sad little Tiny Tim. He was probably glad to get away from our house in case he, too, might see the spirits of Christmases past.

Once, and only once, was I ever taken to the theatre. The disastrous occasion was a visit to the Birmingham Alexandra to see *Mother Goose*. Father's friend from Cadbury's had arranged the outing and for a special treat had booked a box.

This was wonderful. The thought of an event such as this had never even entered my head. So close to the stage were we that when an enormous man called Sammy, dressed in a striped swimsuit and carrying a bucket and spade appeared, he was able to lift me out of the box, put me down on the stage and present me with a bucket full of goodies. It was quite a large bucket and full of sweets – the most I had ever been given.

From that moment on, I was completely stage-struck and determined to become an actress. But Fate had set its seal for me. My destiny was all fixed. Ten minutes later I was removed to the 'ladies' in disgrace. The whole event had proved too much for me. I scarcely understood what all the fuss was about. After all, I had only leaned over the box and hit the violinist on the head with my spade. Perhaps that was why he wasn't too pleased. But it *had* been an accident . . . at least I think it had!

75

The Coventry Carol

The ancient Coventry Carol, with its familiar haunting tune, originated in the fifteenth century as part of Coventry's Pageant of the Shearmen and Tailors. *It provided a fittingly poignant background to the scene in which Herod's soldiers arrive to slay the innocent children, and survives to this day as a favourite among the traditional carols at Christmastime.*

O Sisters too, how may we do
For to preserve this day,
This poor youngling
For whom we do sing,
By by, lul-ly lul-lay?

Herod the king,
In his raging,
Charged he hath this day
His men of might,
In his own sight,
All young children to slay.

That woe is me,
Poor child for thee!
And ever morn and day,
For thy parting
Neither say nor sing
By by, lul-ly lul-lay!

Lul-ly, lul-la, thou little tiny child,
By by, lul-ly lul-lay.

The Christmas Dinner

WASHINGTON IRVING

This second extract from Irving's The Sketch Book of Geoffrey Crayon, Gent. *describes the traditions surrounding the festive dinner on Christmas Day at Bracebridge Hall, seen through the eyes of a house-guest who was staying there at the invitation of Squire Bracebridge's son Frank. Irving, who probably based his fictional mansion on Aston Hall in Birmingham, liberally laced his essays with poetic quotations. This passage is introduced by lines from Wither's 'Juvenilia'.*

Lo, now is come our joyful'st feast!
Let every man be jolly;
Eache roome with yvie leaves is drest,
And every post with holly.
Now all our neighbours' chimneys smoke,
And Christmas blocks are burning;
Their ovens they with bak't meats choke,
And all their spits are turning.
Without the door let sorrow lie,
And if, for cold, it hap to die,
We'll bury 't in a Christmas pye,
And evermore be merry.

I had finished my toilet, and was loitering with Frank Bracebridge in the library, when we heard a distinct thwacking sound, which he informed me was a signal for the serving up of the dinner. The squire kept up old customs in kitchen as well as hall, and the rolling-pin, struck upon the dresser by the cook, summoned the servants to carry in the meats.

The dinner was served up in the great hall, where the squire always held his Christmas banquet. A blazing crackling fire of logs had been heaped on to warm the spacious apartment, and the flame went sparkling and wreathing up the wide-mouthed chimney. The great picture of the crusader and his white horse had been profusely decorated with greens for the occasion; and holly and ivy had likewise been wreathed round the helmet and weapons on the opposite wall, which I understood were the arms of the same warrior.

A sideboard was set out just under this chivalric trophy, on which was a display of plate that might have vied (at least in variety) with Belshazzar's parade of the vessels of the temple: flagons, cans, cups, beakers, goblets, basins and ewers; the gorgeous utensils of good companionship that had gradually accumulated through many generations of jovial housekeepers. Before these stood the two yule candles, beaming like two stars of the first magnitude; other lights were distributed in branches, and the whole array glittered like a firmament of silver.

We were ushered into this banqueting scene with the sound of minstrelsy, the old harper being seated on a stool beside the fireplace, and twanging his instrument with a vast deal more power than melody.

Never did Christmas board display a more goodly and gracious assemblage of countenances; those who were not handsome were, at least, happy; and happiness is a rare improver of your hard-favoured visage.

· A Warwickshire Christmas ·

The parson said grace, which was not a short familiar one, such as is commonly addressed to the Deity in these unceremonious days; but a long, courtly well-worded one of the ancient school. There was now a pause, as if something was expected; when suddenly the butler entered the hall with some degree of bustle. He was attended by a servant on each side with a large wax-light, and bore a silver dish, on which was an enormous pig's head, decorated with rosemary, with a lemon in its mouth, which was placed with great formality at the head of the table. The moment this pageant made its appearance, the harper struck up a flourish; at the conclusion of which, the young Oxonian, on receiving a hint from the squire, gave, with an air of the most comic gravity, an old carol, the first verse of which was as follows:

> Caput apri defero,
> Reddens laudes Domino.
> The boar's head in hand bring I,
> With garlands gay and rosemary.
> I pray you all synge merily
> Qui estis in convivio.

Though prepared to witness many of these little eccentricities, from being apprized of the peculiar hobby of mine host; yet, I confess, the parade with which so odd a dish was introduced somewhat perplexed me, until I gathered from the conversation of the squire and the parson, that it was meant to represent the bringing in of the boar's head; a dish formerly served up with much ceremony and the sound of minstrelsy and song, at great tables, on Christmas Day.

The table was literally loaded with good cheer, and presented an epitome of country abundance, in this season of overflowing larders. A distinguished post was allotted to 'ancient sirloin', as mine host termed it; being, as he added,

· A Warwickshire Christmas ·

Winter at Aston Hall in Birmingham, the Jacobean mansion
on which it is thought Washington Irving based
Bracebridge Hall

'the standard of old English hospitality, and a joint of goodly
presence, and full of expectation'. There were several dishes
quaintly decorated, and which had evidently something traditional in their embellishments; but about which, as I did not
like to appear over-curious, I asked no questions.

I could not, however, but notice a pie, magnificently
decorated with peacock's feathers, in imitation of the tail of
that bird, which overshadowed a considerable tract of the
table. This the squire confessed with some little hesitation,
was a pheasant pie, though a peacock pie was certainly the
most authentical; but there had been such a mortality among
the peacocks this season, that he could not prevail upon
himself to have one killed.

80

I was pleased however to see the respect shown to his whims by his children and relatives; who, indeed, entered readily into the full spirit of them, and seemed all well versed in their parts, having doubtless been present at many a rehearsal. I was amused, too, at the air of profound gravity with which the butler and other servants executed the duties assigned to them, however eccentric. They had an old-fashioned look; having, for the most part, been brought up in the household, and grown into keeping with the antiquated mansion, and the humours of its lord; and most probably looked upon all his whimsical regulations as the established laws of honourable house-keeping.

When the cloth was removed, the butler brought in a huge silver vessel of rare and curious workmanship, which he placed before the squire. Its appearance was hailed with acclamation; being the Wassail Bowl, so renowned in Christmas festivity. The contents had been prepared by the squire himself; for it was a beverage in the skilful mixture of which he particularly prided himself; alleging that it was too abstruse and complex for comprehension of an ordinary servant. It was a potation, indeed, that might well make the heart of a toper leap within him; being composed of the richest and raciest wines, highly spiced and sweetened, with roasted apples bobbing about the surface.

The old gentleman's whole countenance beamed with a serene look of indwelling delight, as he stirred this mighty bowl. Having raised it to his lips, with a hearty wish of a merry Christmas to all present, he sent it brimming round the board, for every one to follow his example, according to the primitive style; pronouncing it 'the ancient fountain of good-feeling, where all hearts met together'.

There was much laughing and rallying as the honest emblem of Christmas circulated, and was kissed rather coyly by the ladies.

The dinner-time passed away in this flow of innocent hilarity; and though the old hall may have resounded in its time with many a scene of broader rout and revel, yet I doubt whether it ever witnessed more honest and genuine enjoyment.

How easy it is for one benevolent being to diffuse pleasure around him; and how truly is a kind heart a fountain of gladness, making everything in its vicinity to freshen into smiles! The joyous disposition of the worthy squire was perfectly contagious; he was happy himself, and disposed to make all the world happy; and the little eccentricities of his humour did but season, in a manner, the sweetness of his philanthropy.

Carols in the Castle

The rugged stone walls of Warwick Castle, and the lofty towers that rise above them, have witnessed the unfolding of many a chequered chapter in English history. Indeed the castle itself is an indelible part of that history, standing majestically at the very heart of England, as a unique symbol of our heritage.

It is in this timeless setting, within the castle's great courtyard, that each year one of Warwickshire's most delightful Christmas traditions takes place to raise funds for charity: Carols in the Castle.

· A Warwickshire Christmas ·

Warwick Castle as depicted in an engraving of 1814

Let us capture the atmosphere as hundreds upon hundreds of local people wind their way up the long castle drives and through the great arched gateway to congregate in the courtyard and join together in the celebration of Christmas.

Many of them carry lanterns, for the night is dark, and the ancient courtyard soon becomes a sea of bobbing lights and flitting shadows. Round about, glowing braziers provide welcome oases of warmth, and there are stalls dispensing hot soup, roast chestnuts and potatoes, mince pies and punch, for there is frost in the night air.

From somewhere comes the strident screech of one of the castle's resident peacocks, no doubt affronted by this unaccustomed nocturnal invasion of its territory.

Then, as the last of the people arrive to swell the throng, an expectant hush descends upon the scene as a spotlight falls on the red-robed members of the choir of St Mary's Church, and a band strikes up the familiar opening notes of 'Once in Royal David's City'.

Soon a great surge of Christmas sound echoes round the castle walls, rises to the floodlit battlements and spills out into the cold night. 'Hark the Herald Angels Sing', 'Good King Wenceslas', 'O Come All Ye Faithful' – the familiar carols ring out in joyful celebration. Interspersed among the traditional favourites are lesser-known Christmas songs performed by the choir alone, and for these the great assembly is hushed in appreciation.

All too soon the final carol is sung, and the crowd, buoyant with the spirit of Christmas, slowly makes its way home. For just a few short hours, the castle will take a rest. Tomorrow, there will be more visitors to swell the hundreds of thousands who come here on 364 days each year.

On just one day is the old castle left alone to its memories – and its peacocks – and that's Christmas Day.

from

Warwickshire Countryside Reflections

ROY WEEKS

In the 1970s, Roy Weeks wrote two delightful and perceptive books portraying the sights and sounds of nature in the county he loved and knew so well. In Warwickshire Countryside Reflections, *he chronicled a year of rural life, season by season, and this extract comes from his observations on winter and Christmastime.*

Whilst the starry canopy of the night was still drawn across the sky, tower and steeple everywhere rang out peal after peal into the quiet atmosphere of another Christmas morning.

Whenever I hear these rousing sounds, I often wonder what degree of jubilation would be acclaimed had the Christmas story evolved around this country, instead of Palestine. Had Warwickshire been allowed to feature in this manner, then I can think of no likelier place to set the scenes than the Southam area. Here, much of the countryside is sparse and

A Warwickshire lane transformed by snow into a winter
picture

inclined to be lonely, particularly the sheep-flecked hillsides in
the vicinity of Priors Marston, and for this reason they could
adequately provide the opening chapters.

Again, the centuries-old market town of Southam could
well be chosen to fill the dramatic rôle. Because of the
characteristic make-up of its streets, the whole appearance
lends itself beautifully to suit all the events which followed. . . .

Now only too soon, this much-prepared-for day begins to
fade, but we like it, not only for what it means to us and the
fact that it makes children of us all, but because it is almost at
the turning-point of the year. It brings us nearer to the early
signs of spring, and lengthening days. Although at the

moment the countryside may have a bleak look about it, there are odd surprises to see.

We notice the grey hazel catkins trembling in the slightest wind, and young honeysuckle leaves boldly trying to relieve the stark hedgerows of their drabness. Over the wheatfields we hear the skylark. He sings of course most of the year, but now, especially, we find his notes a welcome sound.

The trees, naked though they are, make a pleasant study etched against the sky. If we get a burst of sunlight playing on a group of silver birches, isolating them against a dark woodland background, and the hunt splashing scarlet amongst the tawny acres, all of it makes a stirring picture to liven a winter's day.

Twelfth Night brings an end to the festival of Christmas. Down come the gay sprigs of holly to be burnt, and away go the decorations for another year.

Looking out into a world of stinging blizzard and mounting drifts, it is hard to realize that on Sunday we shall be thinking about the fields and the sowing of seed, when the plough is brought into church to be blessed. To this simple act of dedication, come not only the ploughmen, but all who share in the task of husbandry. The millers attend too, as well as the people who bake the bread.

Years ago, Plough Monday was an important event in the calendar. Ploughmen did not work on that day; instead, they processed around the village with a ribbon-bedecked plough. They collected alms to pay for the 'plough candles' which were kept burning all day in the churches symbolizing prayer for a bountiful harvest. Some parts of the day, like many of our old customs, was spent in revelry and jollification.

To most of us, a tractor-drawn plough is a commonplace feature of the landscape, but it is surprising the number of farm workers there are, of the older generation of course, who can recall most vividly their experiences of the days when

horses were extensively used for ploughing. The mention of such lovely creatures as Shires, Clydesdales and Suffolk Punches, causes them to lapse into nostalgic reverie.

I can only remember seeing ploughing with horses on one or two occasions. It was an unforgettable experience – theirs was the finest example of teamwork that I had ever seen. Nevertheless, whether the plough was horse-pulled or mechanically-aided, the very sight of shiny pleats of turned earth, made up for a lot of winter's isolation.

from

Our Old Home

NATHANIEL HAWTHORNE

Nathaniel Hawthorne, the nineteenth-century American author, served as his country's consul in Liverpool. He travelled extensively in Britain, and for a time had a house in Leamington Spa. In this passage from Our Old Home, *he recalls a winter's visit to Warwick during which he is taken on a guided tour of the historic Lord Leycester Hospital and the adjoining chapel of St James, still one of the county town's most familiar landmarks.*

· A Warwickshire Christmas ·

The day, though it began brightly, had long been overcast, and the clouds now spat down a few spiteful drops upon us. Besides that, the east wind was very chill; so we descended the winding tower-stair, and went next into the garden, one side of which is shut in by almost the only remaining portion of the old city wall.

From the garden we went into the kitchen, where the fire was burning hospitably, and diffused a genial warmth far and wide, together with the fragrance of some old English roast beef, which, I think, must at that moment have been done nearly to a turn.

The kitchen is a lofty, spacious and noble room, partitioned off round the fireplace by a sort of semicircular oaken screen, or rather, an arrangement of heavy and high-backed settles, with an ever open entrance between them, on either side of which is the omnipresent image of the Bear and Ragged Staff, three feet high, and excellently carved in oak, now black with time and unctuous kitchen smoke.

The ponderous mantlepiece, likewise of carved oak, towers high towards the dusky ceiling, and extends its mighty breadth to take in a vast area of hearth, the arch of the fireplace being positively so immense that I could compare it to nothing but the city gateway. Above its cavernous opening were crossed two ancient halberds, the weapons, possibly, of soldiers who had fought under Leicester in the Low Countries; and elsewhere on the walls were displayed several muskets, which some of the present inmates of the hospital may have levelled against the French.

Another ornament of the mantelpiece was a square of silken needlework or embroidery, faded nearly white, but dimly representing that wearisome Bear and Ragged Staff, which we should hardly look twice at, only that it was wrought by the fair fingers of poor Amy Robsart, and beautifully framed in oak from Kenilworth Castle, at the expense of a Mr Conner, a

89

The chapel of St James above the old West Gate at Warwick
adjoining the Lord Leycester Hospital. The county town's
main street is not yet marred by twentieth-century traffic

countryman of our own. Certainly, no Englishman would be
capable of this little bit of enthusiasm.

Finally, the kitchen firelight glistens on a splendid display
of copper flagons, all of generous capacity, and one of them
about as big as half a barrel; the smaller vessels contain the
customary allowance of ale, and the larger one is filled with
that foaming liquor on four festive occasions of the year, and
emptied amain by the jolly brotherhood. I should be glad to
see them do it; but it would be an exploit fitter for Queen
Elizabeth's age than these degenerate times.

The kitchen is the social hall of the twelve brethren. In the
daytime, they bring their little messes to be cooked here, and
eat them in their own parlours; but after a certain hour, the
great hearth is cleared and swept, and the old men assemble
round its blaze, each with his tankard and his pipe, and hold
high converse through the evening.

If the Master be a fit man for his office, methinks he will sometimes sit down sociably among them, for there is an elbow-chair by the fireside which it would not demean his dignity to fill, since it was occupied by King James at the great festival of nearly three centuries ago. A sip of the ale and a whiff of the tobacco-pipe would put him in friendly relations with his venerable household; and then we can fancy him instructing them by pithy apothegms and religious texts which were first uttered here by some Catholic priest, and have impregnated the atmosphere ever since.

The Village Shop

FRED ARCHER

Although Fred Archer has based much of his writing on the village in Worcestershire in which he was brought up on the family farm, his knowledge of rural life and customs cannot be confined within county boundaries. This evocative essay on the traditional village shop and its contribution to the Christmas ritual between the wars gleans its inspiration no less from Warwickshire than from anywhere else.

Although some village shops today are more like mini

supermarkets, with wire baskets stacked up near the door and the shoppers helping themselves off the shelves, I still remember the village shop of yesterday. It was an institution, often combining the Post Office as well, and it ranked in importance with the school, the pub and the church in village life.

Let's peep into a shop of years ago, before there were cars and buses to take us to the multiple stores in the nearest town.

The shelves in the window were lined with jars of sweets – acid drops, pear drops and barley sugar – fused together and having to be parted by the shopkeeper's wooden spoon when a village child asked for four ounces.

A white-aproned man would be standing behind the scrubbed wooden counter. He weighed the sweets on his scales, then made a paper bag by folding a square of paper into a funnel. Into this he dropped the sticky sugary pennyworth for a little boy or girl to enjoy.

For a halfpenny we used to buy a bull's eye or gob-stopper. These hard, round ping-pong balls of sweetness changed colour as they were sucked and were constantly taken from the mouth for inspection until the last morsel revealed a soft centre!

Looking around was an adventure. On the wall the pocket knives took my eye; they were on a card with the expensive ones at the top for the shepherd to pare the sheep's feet or the carter to shape whip sticks, while at the bottom, in my price range, were what were called scout knives with a spike to get stones out of horses' hooves.

Paraffin or lamp oil was supplied from a forty-gallon iron drum with a tap. Alongside was the vinegar barrel, ready for use with its wooden tap to dispense the amber liquid into the beer bottles of the village.

The scent from the selection of cheeses was one to remember. Nearby was the wire used to cut off the sections of cheese,

and I remember that the villagers were allowed a piece about the size of mousetrap bait just to taste and decide if it was too mild or too mature.

Tubs and wooden buckets of butter offered a selection ranging from the very salty to the slightly salty with which to plaster on the cottage loaves.

Nothing was wasted in those days, for when the wooden butter buckets were empty they were sold at 6d a piece to the customers for carrying water and for floor scrubbing.

Bacon boxes fixed on pram wheels made good trucks to bring the potatoes and other vegetables back from the allotment. The bacon itself was cut into rashers with a well-steeled carving knife; there were no cutting machines in those days.

A dear old friend recalls how often was the time she bought two ounces of tea – or even a pennyworth – from the village shop. The tea was weighed on the counter scales fresh from the tea chests. There was Darjeeling, Ceylon, or whatever the locals liked. And how pretty was some of the paper in which the tea was wrapped. The empty tea chests were sold for a few coppers, and these made tolerable chicken coops with a few slats of wood in front.

Cocoa always intrigued me. The well-known brands were said to be pure, but for twopence a packet, an inferior powder, mixed I recall, with cornflour, suited the pocket of many of the folk who were having a job to make ends meet.

All the materials for washday were at hand in the shop too: yellow soap in long bars for washing, Hudson's Powder, soda, Reckitt's Blue and white Windsor soap for toilet use.

I doubt if many village folk chew twist tobacco today, or even smoke it. But in the old days twist was sold to the farmworker by the ounce in long shoe-string pieces. Captain Webb matches at $1\frac{1}{2}$d. a dozen boxes were sold as well. They were named after the first man to swim the Channel.

Village women at Berkswell plucking poultry for sale at
Christmas before the First World War

'Everything in season' was the motto of the man who ran the
stores. He knew that folk grew their own vegetables so didn't
offer any for sale except for dried peas which had to be soaked.
Split peas at a cheaper price were also stocked, and these were
used for soups, stews or broth.

Tinned peas had not yet arrived. In fact, tinned food
generally was almost unknown.

Leather laces for workaday boots and cotton laces for
Sundays; reels of cotton; cards of needles; candles by the
pound; blocks of salt; little blue bags of sugar: all these were
kept in stock. Oranges arrived for Christmas with bags of nuts
and sticky blocks of dates as well.

Christmas time was a short but busy season in the village shop. About a fortnight before 25 December, the window took on a festive look with Japanese lanterns, and it was candle-lit at night. Gauze Christmas stockings hung from the wall, and there were little cardboard Father Christmases peeping out between sugar mice among the cheap toys, tops and celluloid dolls.

It was a Christmas tradition in 'the trade' for all the regular customers to be given a present at Christmas. It might have been a box of biscuits or some sweets for the children.

Behind the counter, the shopkeeper, always clinically clean in his white apron, patted the butter, making the impression of a cow on each pound he worked. Some of the larger village shops had huge mahogany-framed mirrors on one wall bearing advertisements for Pear's soap or Rowntree's cocoa. These mirrors reflected all the goods on the opposite wall giving the shop a feeling of spaciousness.

It's a far cry from those days to the supermarkets of today. It had to change I suppose but for me it seems a bit off to have to push a 'pram load' of groceries around searching for the jam and the tea, and then see the till clocking up figures just in pounds and pence!

Ghosts in Warwickshire

URSULA BLOOM

This third item from the works of Ursula Bloom delves into the world of the supernatural. In her childhood, when she lived in her father's rambling rectory at Whitchurch in southernmost Warwickshire, ghost stories were rife, and people, on the whole, were a good deal less cynical about them than they are today.

Christmas has always been the time of year for ghost stories. I remember, as a small child in Warwickshire, a kitchen maid brought me bread-and-milk in bed, and stayed for an entertaining chat which, I am sure, would have petrified my parents. She apparently knew every ghost in the neighbourhood, and was only too happy to inform me about them.

One of her most intriguing stories was about the ghost of Shakespeare, which walked round the Guild Chapel at Stratford on Christmas night. I've never heard the story from anyone else, and don't believe it's true.

But there came the awful moment when she met a ghost – a real one, so she said, and 'it fair made me shake'. This was, of course, terrifying bedtime chatter for any child, and she was never sparing in her realism. How I ever got to sleep afterwards, I don't know.

· A Warwickshire Christmas ·

She met her real ghost – 'ever so frightening' – in Christmas
week in the Preston lane. This little by-way runs from the
main Shipston–Stratford road, down beside Alscot Park to the
village of Preston-on-Stour. It drops down to the river, crosses
it, then one half of it turns left to the parish of Whitchurch,
where my father was rector, and the other half is a dead-end
road running to Preston itself. An old flailing barn stands at
the corner. Here, apparently, in the dark, this girl met her
ghost, and she thought it was some relation of the 'white lady
of Alscot', a well-known phantom in those parts, which
usually reserved its attentions for Alscot Hall itself.

I sat up in bed in rapt interest. The maid had been coming
home from seeing her grandmother, when she heard someone
behind her. She turned sharply and looked into a pair of the
most beautiful eyes that she had ever seen. But the poor lady's
face, she said, was as white as snow. Then the apparition
turned and moved away. The maid was, of course, all of a
shiver, and utterly horrified. I was very much afraid myself,
though I was safely in bed, with a nice hot brick wrapped in a
duster at my feet.

This story was not reserved only for the maid. My father
found that half the village was scared stiff of that particular
lane on a winter's night, declaring that the ghost was always
there. One night my father set forth with a friend, and the
French master from the Army School at Stratford-upon-Avon
to help him. I wouldn't have taken a Frenchman myself, and of
course this one hadn't really wanted to go. Nevertheless, he
went, lest anyone should think he was a coward. It was he who
actually came face to face with the wraith, by the old flailing
barn. He had turned and found himself staring into the lovely
lustrous eyes of a woman, who was by all accounts, not quite
his height.

Hearing him scream my father went to his rescue and saw
for himself the dead-white face and the lovely eyes. He then

noticed that she turned and ran away. He could hear her feet, and fortunately recognised them as being the feet of a deer escaped from Alscot Park.

At this time of year, it seemed that the deer were always escaping, and the darkness effectively hid their ears and antlers, so that one looked into an unrecognizable face. The wretched animal in the lane on that particular night was making desperate efforts to get back into the park, and, being used to men, instinctively followed human voices to seek help. It was terrifying for those who thought it was a ghost.

'It always happened at Christmastime,' said my informant, who even when told the truth would not believe that it was something as harmless as a deer. For, as she said: 'What she'd bin and gone and seen, had been no deer anyway.' And she added: 'That Alscot Park's haunted.'

This same maid was the person who first told me of the White Lady of Alscot whose habit was to come down the stairs unexpectedly, usually at Christmastime. Apparently she was very well known indeed.

The grandfather of the squire, a naval commander who was celebrating Christmas with the flowing bowl, once saw this lady coming down the stairs in the great hall. He was not afraid of her, and picked up a riding whip and chased her up the stairs again. The next few Christmases were completely peaceful without her intrusions; then it all began again.

It appears that she never did any harm, and apparently did not want anything except to make friends, which was something she had never been able to do.

As a small child I was somewhat naturally intensely interested in ghosts. One Christmas, my father took me to visit an old lady who was having her home decorated for the festive season. I've never seen lovelier holly. She had no mistletoe (in those days it was not popular), perhaps because you had to buy it, whereas Dame Nature gave you all the other

Snow and mist add beauty to Church Avenue in Stratford-
upon-Avon early this century – a winter scene which would
have been familiar to Ursula Bloom and her family

evergreens free. 'But,' said the old lady mysteriously, 'you
always have to decorate with a piece of rosemary as well, for
that keeps the ghosts away!'

I thought that pronouncement was very interesting, and to
be on the safe side I picked a piece of rosemary and took it up
to my own room at the rectory, just to make sure that I had
insured myself against the occult.

Warwick Castle was said to have ghosts galore, though I

have never seen one there at all. I remember a footman asking me if I hadn't heard the ghosts screaming in the night, which I most certainly had not. The peacocks screeching on the battlements at dawn had awakened me, but I knew what was making that appalling din, for my father had warned me of them.

The very old people used to say that the castle was haunted by a black dog. It had started when an old retainer there, a woman called Moll Bloxham, had sold milk and butter from the castle stores for her personal gain. One Christmas she overdid this, and the then Earl of Warwick, getting wind of it, had stopped her source of supply.

Furiously angry, she vowed she would 'get them haunted'. She apparently succeeded and returned in the form of a big black dog. In the end, the clergy were called in to exorcise the ghost with bell, book and candle, but for a time they were entirely unsuccessful. Then, one day, it was said that a huge black dog sprang from Caesar's Tower into the river below, and so ended the ghost story.

Although one rather expected Christmas ghosts in this part of the world during that delightful era, I must admit that, after going to some enthralling party and driving back ten miles through the dank darkness of those Warwickshire lanes, sitting inside a hired 'fly' which smelt of mothballs, it could be a little horrifying if one had been talking of the supernatural. One wondered if one dare ask mother if the stories were really true.

Some years later, I did run into a ghost myself, and although you may not believe me, I don't really care, for I know it happened. And I know another thing about it; I am never taking the risk of it happening again.

My mother and I had been into Stratford on bicycles to attend a Christmas pantomime, written and produced by the famous Bruce Bairnsfather. It was a very lively show, for he

could be extremely witty. We were cycling back home far later than we had planned (the stable clock at Alscot struck the hour of midnight as we passed by the gates). I went ahead down the lane. By the first gate I found a man walking in the gutter towards the village, and I nearly ran over him. It happened again a few yards further on, so I called back to my mother, thinking she might run into one of them herself.

Then, quite suddenly, I got the jitters. I was ice-cold when I reached home. It was absurd to feel so upset, because we had had a wonderful evening. We were in the Christmas mood, and the men I had seen in the lane were probably ordinary men, who had perhaps been out to some entertainment like ourselves. (Most likely at the Bell at Alderminster!)

Next day, I made some enquiries, and I always got the same curious answer: Surely I knew that a man had committed suicide by setting his horse at the gate to that field and had died here in the hard winter of 1882? Did I not know that he came back at midnight – the hour of his deed – and that no-one in the village would ever go down the lane at that time of night, because they knew he was – as they expressed it – hanging about?

What I did know was that after I had met him, I had been more scared than ever before in my life. I certainly shan't be coming down that lane at that hour ever again.

'Be careful of ghosts,' said the little maid who brought me up my bread-and-milk in bed. She certainly had a point there.

Christmas at Aston Hall

CHARLES LINES

In earlier pages are two accounts of Christmas celebrations at Washington Irving's fictional Bracebridge Hall, a mansion thought to have been based on Aston Hall in Birmingham. But the real Aston Hall also had its traditional Christmases. Charles Lines wrote this account in 1970.

Aston Hall is now within the confines of Birmingham, with stark blocks of flats, the Aston Villa ground and giant cooling-towers forming part of a largely incongruous setting that seems merely to emphasize the beauty of the place.

Certainly, the Christmas festivities, which Irving delighted in, such as the squire's dish of 'frumenty' – 'wheat cakes boiled in milk, with rich spices' – the mummers and carols, the wassail bowl and the procession to church, would all have been part and parcel of the festive season at the grand house on the hill.

A curious Christmas Eve custom at Aston Hall is also mentioned by the *Gentleman's Magazine* in 1795: 'As soon as supper is over, a table is set in the hall; a brown loaf with twenty-three silver threepences stuck on the top of it; a tankard of ale, with pipes and tobacco; and the two oldest

· A Warwickshire Christmas ·

Aston Hall, scene of festive celebrations both traditional and curious

servants have chairs behind it, to sit as judges, if they please. The steward brings the servants, both men and women, by one at a time, covered with a winnow sheet, and lays their right hand on the loaf, exposing no other part of the body; the older of the two judges guesses at the person, by naming a name, then the younger judge, and lastly the older one again.

'If they hit upon the right name, the steward leads the person back again; but if they do not, he takes off the winnow sheet, and the person receives a threepence, makes a low obeisance to the judges, but speaks not a word.'

All the servants were brought in, but 'whatever servant had not slept in the house the preceding night, forfeited his right to the money. . . . When the money is gone, the servants have full liberty to dance, sing, and go to bed when they please.'

Even at this distance of time, it is not too difficult to hear in one's imagination the sounds of children's games, or 'God Rest You Merry, Gentlemen', in the long gallery upstairs; to

103

picture reflected firelight on moulded ceilings and sombre wainscot. There are, of course, occasions when festivities still take place there, candlelight sometimes bestowing a mellow glow upon the tapestries and, glinting from every window, even to the turrets, turning the mansion into a sort of fairytale castle in the most unlikely of situations.

Epitaph to a Carpenter

JAMES SARGEANT

In contrast to the earlier Warwick epitaph to the Countess of Leicester, who died on Christmas Day in 1634, this one at Northfield Church in Birmingham has a faintly humorous ring about it. James Sargeant, a nailer, carpenter and joiner who was born on Christmas Day in 1718, composed it himself in preparation for his own death, engraving it on a stone which he embellished with the tools of his trade. He left a space for the date of his death to be added, and this was duly done — 13 January 1799, aged 80 years. One hopes he was a better carpenter than he was a poet.

104

I was born on Christmas Day,
My parents were so glad of me
That to the wise man they did go
The future of my birth to know;
He said ingenious I should be,
So a good trade provide for me;
So to the nail block I was set
As if the Lord they meant to fret,
Which I pursued until 23,
Then seven years sawing was for me.
Then with the plane and other tools
My God directed me to use,
For what was offered me to do,
My heart and hands could go through.

Christmas in the 'Good Old Days'

GILBERT MOORE

When, in 1965, Gilbert Moore wrote this evocation of a
Victorian Christmas in Birmingham, he looked back a
century and took the year 1865 as his focus. It was a time

· A Warwickshire Christmas ·

*of great affluence, as the city's industrial and commercial
importance burgeoned. For the many under-privileged, it
was also a time of incredible poverty and hardship.*

Set fair for a Merry Christmas and a Happy New Year, it was
boom time in Birmingham in 1865. No other town of its size
in England enjoyed more material comfort. A reliable work-
man in any of its principal trades could be sure of 30s. a week,
many in the brass trade earned 40s. to 50s., while the
plutocrats of the gun trade could make as much as £5 and £6
per week.

For the most part thrifty, they invested their savings in the
Penny Bank, or one of the innumerable benefit societies
connected with the churches and chapels, in the Oddfellows
and the Foresters, or less prudently in money clubs attached to
the public houses.

As it happened, only that April many savings had been in
the balance when, in the commercial bank panic, Attwood's
and the Penny Banks collapsed. Public subscription, led by
such families as the Chances and the Barrows, and by firms like
Heaton Taylor and the Birmingham Banking Company,
retrieved the losses to some extent; and by the end of the year,
most of Birmingham was looking forward to a Christmas in
keeping with its affluence.

But in an age which expected the poor to be always with
them and everyone to know their station, there were inevitably
Ragged Robins. The worst of them, crowded about Steelhouse
Lane and in the area between New Street and Temple Row
known as The Gullet, lived in conditions that, in a few years'
time, were to become a national scandal.

For them, the Christmas celebrations of 1865 were confined
to a wistful journey through the gaslit glitter of Bull Street,
New Street and the High Street, pressing their cold noses to
the elegant windows of Crockford Grove, which were filled

· *A Warwickshire Christmas* ·

'The King of the Peacocks', a scene from a Victorian
Christmas show entitled *Splendiferous* at Day's Birmingham
Crystal Palace Concert Hall

with cascades of ribbon and book muslin; staring at the latest
in French, evening and ball gowns which Mrs Howe of Bull
Street had 'just received from her Paris agent'. They could only
try to imagine the joy of the 'Very Pleasing and Astonishing
Chemical Toys' which, when lighted, burst into bouquets of
roses, into butterflies and serpents; or giggle outside the
Original Stay Warehouse in the High Street, with its formidable whale-bone corsets, its assortments of crinolines and
made-to-measure stays. They gazed at such mouth-watering
displays of prime beef, turkeys and geese, fruit and chestnuts
as they had never known, and were tantalized by the array of
Cluny lace in S. and N. Cooke's; by the Melton, Elgin and
Whitney coats available from Davis and Co. at a guinea

upwards. And, oh for one of those children's Inverness capes at 5s. 6d. to keep out the easterly wind!

Outside the Theatre Royal in New Street, the playbills were all the ragamuffins were likely to see of *Harlequin, Sinbad and the Red Dwarfs*. There, Mr and Mrs Average of Brum, the gun trade and the button men, the enamellers and jewellers, the hollow-ware and bedstead makers, were about to enter the theatre. Indulgently, they tossed the urchins a copper or two, and the lucky ones scuttled back to their smallpox-ridden, diphtheria-haunted tenements between the back gardens of New Street and St Philip's Church, to recount to those too sick or aged to move, the magical wonder of the Birmingham without.

Meanwhile, back at the Royal, Mr Average in his guinea Melton coat and the Little Woman in her crinoline and Original Stays, were ensconced in the 1s. stalls, enjoying 'the Capital Scenic Effects; the Delightful Transformation Scenes'. Others of their station at the Prince of Wales, were absorbed in *Bo Peep or Harlequin Butterfly's Ball*, while at Day's Crystal Palace they were tickled by Mr McCarthy, 'the Arkansas comedian and vocalist'. The more pretentious among them spent a genteel evening at Holder's Music Hall watching popular ballet, where, during the interval, Mr Johnny Day, the world champion walker, demonstrated his prowess by walking a mile back and forth across the stage in nine minutes.

Those who liked 'good' music enjoyed a popular concert at the Exchange Assembly Rooms, while others favoured the Atheneum Hall in Temple Street where there were soirées at the Shakespeare Restaurant, open till 12 midnight.

But the great majority of those who indulged in commercial entertainment that Christmas week went to Aston Lower Grounds, recently opened by Queen Victoria, and where in the Assembly Rooms there was Father Christmas and the Wassail Bowl, and dancing and singing till midnight. So great was the

A Christmas blizzard hits the streets of Birmingham in
1869. It seems that roadworks were as much a problem at
that time as they are today

attendance that special trains were laid on to take visitors from
New Street Station to Aston.

At the Town Hall that week, a notable violinist, Mr
Anderton, gave a concert. Some days previously it had been
announced with pride that the reservations of every seat in the
gallery and a large proportion of the floor had 'secured the
countenance and support of our aristoracy'. From the heights
of Edgbaston and the limitless greenery of Calthorpe Park they
came, in carriage and hansom, the Master groomed with
Rowland's Macassar Oil, 'invigorating and beautifying beyond
all precedence', his Good Lady also beautified by courtesy of
Rowland's with their Kalydor Complexion Cream, her entire
ensemble made of the fashionable Velours de Londres.

As the carriages circled the Town Hall, depositing their charges, Mr and Mrs Average regarded their betters with an unctuous pride, while an occasional urchin who may have escaped the back of the Bobby's hand, gazed in disbelief at the other half of the world of Brum.

The Town Hall was again the pivot of society when a ball was held there on Boxing Day, and Mrs Howe's elegant French ball gowns became animated by the 'Rhine Wine Lancers', the 'Florence Valse' and the 'Mayfair Gallop', as the 'admirers of the Terpsichorean Revels footed it on the light fantastic toe right merrily'. Afterwards, for those who wished, a ball supper was available at Lisseters Restaurant, recently established by the late cook of the Reform Club.

But as far as Christmas Day itself was concerned, the differences were not so great. There was plenty of prime beef and plum pudding in the town for most levels of society, the main distinction being in the variety and refinement of the 'trimmings'; between sherry at 24s. and 50s. per dozen, and claret at 14s. and 20s. Champagne could not be bought at less that 43s. per dozen, but Old Irish Whiskey and gin were more or less standard at about 18s. per dozen and 13s.4d. per gallon respectively. For the aftermath, Doctor Coffin's Indian Stomach Pills and Mrs Winslow's Soothing Syrup were available to all at the same price.

As the *Birmingham Journal* reported: 'Christmas fare has never been more inviting, nor the shops more resplendent. Christmas boxes circulated as freely as bad halfpennies; hampers flew about like property loaves in a pantomime'.

That week, charitable attention was given to 407 inmates of the asylum, 2,000 of the workhouse, 185 tramps and 8,300 out-of-door poor.

It had, indeed, been a Dickens of a Christmas.

Christmas in Ettington

MARY ROSE HAYFIELD

Born in Marston Green when it was still a village, and long before it became overshadowed by Birmingham International Airport, Mary Rose Hayfield admits that communing with nature has always played a vital rôle in her life. She expresses her deep love of the Warwickshire countryside in verse, simple but sincere, and it is from her collection Beloved Warwickshire *that these seasonal lines are taken.*

There's a light in the vicarage window
And it shines on the path to the door,
Which is left on the latch as you enter,
So you know that your welcome is sure.

There's a light by the tree in the church now,
And the presents piled high all around
Are the tokens of love from our children
To others, whose joy shall abound.

There's a light by the crib in the church now,
And Mary and Joseph are there
With the lambs and the little brown donkey
And the Baby, whose name is a prayer.

111

There's a light in the village at Christmas
And it's there in all things that we do.
It's the spirit of loving and giving;
May it stay with us all the year through.

Christmas Comes
but Once a Year

FRED ARCHER

*Fred Archer's second seasonal contribution is a delightful
mixture of personal memories and ancient customs, a
characteristic literary blend he so often puts to good effect in
his many books and articles.*

Long dark nights and cold cheerless days remind us that
St Thomas's Day, 21 December, is the shortest day of the
year. Folk today who live in centrally-heated houses without
fireplaces miss something of the sounds of winter. When we
hear the wind growling in the chimney and having an
argument with the doors and windows, it gives a feeling of
comfort that we have the blessing of a good roof over our head,
and a warm and comfortable hearth. Thoughts of the gale

· A Warwickshire Christmas ·

The age-old custom of gathering greenery for Christmas

outside give a peculiar sense of pleasure, and the logs on the fire really do sing and provide an ever-changing picture:

> Outside fall the snow flakes lightly,
> Through the night loud raves the storm.
> In my room the fire glows brightly
> And 'tis cosy, silent, warm.
> Musing sit I on the settle
> By the firelight's cheerful blaze,
> Listening to the busy kettle,
> Humming long forgotten lays.

Evergreens have always brightened the countryside at Christmas – the holly and the ivy, and of course the mistletoe. I'm, especially fond of ivy, as its dark green shines when the hedges and trees are bare. When a withy tree by the brookside is capped with ivy, it gives a bountiful feast to the wood

113

pigeons. They love the berries in the hungry winter months when the cabbage and clover fields are covered with snow.

Long before the Christian era, our ancestors decorated their houses with greenery at the winter solstice. We also read in the Bible how Nehemiah ordered the people during a festive season 'to go unto the mount and fetch branches of the trees and make green arbours. Every one upon the roof of his house, in their courts, and in the courts of the house of God.'

Virgil wrote that the practice of trimming the temples with hanging flowers, boughs and garlands was taken from the heathen people who decked their idols and houses with such array.

A later writer, Chandler, says of the Celts: 'Their houses and temples were decked with evergreens in December, that the spirits of the woods might repair to them and remain unnipped with frosts and cold winds until a milder season.'

Mistletoe, which is a parasite, grows mostly on gnarled apple trees, although some of the best berried branches I have found have been on a hawthorn bush. Sometimes it grows on the large boughs at the top of poplar trees which are tantalizingly out of reach.

It has long been the custom to wait until Christmas Eve before the mistletoe bough is brought into the house. Today, markets in many a Warwickshire town still do a roaring trade in mistletoe in the days immediately before Christmas.

Why is mistletoe so often banned from church decorations at Christmas time? Is it supersitition? There was an occasion some years ago when a sexton put mistletoe among the evergreens to decorate the church, but the parson said that as it was an unholy plant used by the Druids in their mystic ceremonies, it was deemed by the church as unhallowed and totally unfit for sacred purposes.

Christmas has always meant a time for feasting. People today don't often overeat and drink like they used to do.

· A Warwickshire Christmas ·

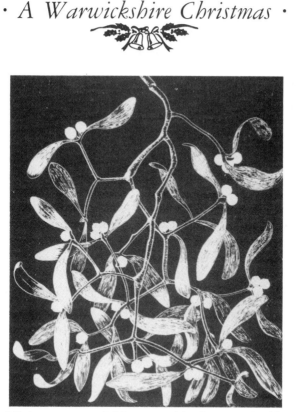

Mistletoe, surrounded by superstition but an essential
Christmas decoration

Nowadays turkey can be bought all the year round; it's not
such a treat as it was. One man I knew traditionally had a
suckling pig for his family's Christmas dinner. He told me
they ate it until they were sick of it, and that he buried the
remainder of it in the garden! Come to think of it, I can also
recall a Warwickshire couple who spent fifty pounds for a fancy
Christmas dinner at a hotel, and were ill all Boxing Day.

My old friend Alf Baker was a different case altogether. He
once told me he had two sausages for his Christmas dinner, but
added, 'It's going to be different next year.' I told him I was
glad to hear it, and asked him what he meant. 'Yes, I'm
having three sausages next year,' he said triumphantly.

An old man who once worked for me was not allowed to smoke or drink. These were his wife's orders. He and his wife went away to their daughter's home for Christmas, and when it was all over I asked him what sort of a Christmas he had had. He replied: 'All right; I smoked a fag in front of the Missus!'.

I always like William Barnes's *Christmas Invitation*:

> Come down tomorrow night and mind
> Don't leave the fiddle bag behind.
> We'll shake a leg and drink a cup
> Of ale and keep old Christmas up.
> And every one shall tell his tale,
> And every one shall sing his song,
> And every one will drink his ale
> To love and friendship all night long.

That's what Christmas is all about: peace and goodwill to all men. It should be a leveller when, perhaps only for a few days, all mankind is equal.

Another Side to Santa Claus

VIVIAN BIRD

*The unlikely and the unexpected have always appealed to
Vivian Bird, even when he is writing on a subject as
familiar as Father Christmas.*

Santa Claus still manages to be his customary benevolent self
each Christmas, although since 1976 he could have been
excused a slight cynicism following his relegation in that year
to a lower status in the Church's calendar.

How many people, I wonder, know that he is also the
patron saint of pawnbrokers?

As a bishop in Asia Minor, Nicholas once saved three children
from being fried by an unscrupulous innkeeper to feed the bishop's
retinue – an act which made him the patron saint of children. At
Beaudesert church in Henley-in-Arden, on the windvane, and in
windows in St Mary's at Warwick and in Willoughby parish
church, Nicholas appears with the three children.

Learning of a good Christian unable to afford a dowry for his
three daughters, Nicholas went, stealthily by night, and left
three bags of gold for the family – thus becoming Santa
Claus, who visits children in some continental countries on
St Nicholas's Day, the 6th December. The three bags of gold,
which can be seen in church windows at Curdworth and

St Nicholas – Santa Claus – is depicted in the left-hand
panel of this window in Willoughby parish church

Dunchurch in Warwickshire, became corrupted into three apples
by artists unsure of what they were copying – as in Alcester church.

In other artists' hands these apples became the golden apples
of legend, from which it was a short step to three golden balls
as at Kenilworth and Ladbroke. Thus St Nicholas was
unwittingly invested with the badge of the money-lending
Medici family, three golden balls, which pawnbrokers had
already adopted as their sign.

So now, finding a saint with the same symbol, they adopted
him – and Father Christmas became the patron saint of
pawnbrokers.

A Charlecote Christmas

SALLY ROWAT

The Christmas season was always celebrated in style at Charlecote Park, the family home of the Lucys, and later the Fairfax-Lucys, near Stratford-upon-Avon. There are records of elaborate Christmas parties in the last century, when Squire Henry Spencer Lucy dressed up as Santa Claus and distributed presents to the village children, but it is the early Christmases of the present century which are recalled here. Sally Rowat recorded these reminiscences in 1975, in conversation with Dr Alianore Fairfax-Lucy, a daughter of the house, who would have been a teenager at Charlecote in the years before the First World War.

The family's gift of a haunch of venison to the parishioners was a traditional Christmas custom. Deer have been kept in the Park since the sixteenth century, and one legend records how Shakespeare was caught poaching them and fined by Sir Thomas Lucy, whom he later characterized as Justice Shallow in *The Merry Wives of Windsor*.

'A few days before Christmas,' Dr Lucy explained, 'large sheets were spread on the surface of the great table in the servants' hall, where a roaring fire burned. The haunches, larded over with fat, were brought in and laid there, each one

· *A Warwickshire Christmas* ·

An old tradition at Charlecote was that the family served at
table when the servants had their Christmas dinner

bearing a little skewer with the name of the recipient. As the
villagers processed through, armed with a bit of sheeting in
which to receive their Christmas gift, Mother and Father stood
there and wished them all a Happy Christmas.'

Then, on Christmas Eve, there was the annual carol singing
ritual. Today, there is no choir at Charlecote, but then, with
some forty village children to swell the ranks, the carollers
produced a merry sound. Firstly, they would walk up the long
drive to the great house and, having sung their fill, would be
presented with hot mince pies and mulled ale for their trouble
– and a donation for the tin for their efforts. Then they'd be off
to the large farms in the area, walking miles up lanes and over
fields to spread their tidings of great joy.

· *A Warwickshire Christmas* ·

Stockings always greeted Christmas morning for the Fairfax-Lucy children. After breakfast, it was a walk across the Park to church; the entire family, plus servants. At that time, the contingent of staff had dwindled since the great days of Squire Spencer, but still consisted of a butler, two footmen, an odd-job man, a cook, kitchen maid, two housemaids, a ladies' maid, nursery maid and governess, three stablemen and two or more gardeners.

'Mother always said this wasn't a house for women "downstairs",' Dr Lucy told me. 'She had been brought up with manservants, to open the heavy shutters, to carry the hot water to the bedrooms – there was no modernization then – and to bring in the logs for all the fires.'

Back at the house after the service, final preparations for Christmas dinner got under way – but not for the family. 'It was always a tradition that *we* waited on the servants and gave them their lunch,' Dr Lucy remembered, 'and then our parents – and the children when we were old enough – ate our Christmas dinner in the evening.'

She described the scene in the great servants' hall, in the early Victorian south wing addition of Charlecote, with its three vast windows overlooking the meandering Avon. A roaring fire burned in the hearth, stags' heads surveyed the scene below, and in the centre of it all stood the vast elm refectory table with benches either side. For once, the 'downstairs' pecking order – which decreed that normally the cook and butler, the ladies' maid and housekeeper ate alone, waited on by the remainder of the staff – went by the board. The entire staff, dressed in crisply starched aprons and pressed uniforms, sat down together to enjoy their annual Christmas treat. And the Fairfax-Lucy family, parents and children, served them with turkey and beef, with plum pudding and bread and cheese and, of course, with ale.

When all were replete, they sat awhile chatting: out came

the clay pipes, and as they revelled in this reversal of rôles, the children of the house washed up. 'Many's the time I spent Christmas afternoon with my hands in the sink,' laughed Dr Lucy.

What then? How did the children fill in the hours before dinner or bedtime? Dr Lucy found it hard to remember: certainly, she said, there were no organized family festive games. They may have sat around the Christmas tree in the Great Hall for a time, or have played hide-and-seek up and down the turrets of the house, a popular game when they were all young. And then again, they may have disappeared into the Park, to run off their high spirits after all that washing up.

Finally, in the evening, the family ate *their* Christmas fare. The smaller children were sent up to bed at 6.30 but the elders remained with their parents in the small dining room of the house (the great dining room was only used for large dinner parties, when the gold plate was used, or for shooting parties).

Here they enjoyed a similar repast to that served earlier in the day to their 'downstairs' family, with whom they enjoyed a close relationship, and with whom deep and lasting friendships sprang up.

The family knew them all intimately; most stayed for life and when they died a son or daughter took their place. They were in their own way privileged, regarded as an extension of the family.

Today, a few can still remember with nostalgia the time when carol singing and hot mince pies, haunches of venison wrapped in scraps of sheet, parties in the Great Hall for starry-eyed village children, and dinner served by the Fairfax-Lucy family to their servants, meant that it was Christmas again at Charlecote Park.

Christmas in the Beginning

LESLIE THOMAS

Leslie Thomas lived in the rural heartland of south Warwickshire near Shipston-on-Stour, amid countryside which was near and dear to his heart. He was a knowledgeable writer on farming and the great outdoors, with a refreshingly anecdotal style. Shortly before he died in 1984, he penned these thoughts about Christmas.

The roots of Christmas, long before Christmas was known, lie in the land, when early man looked up at the sky at the winter solstice and noted the waxing and waning of the sun. Yule, I believe, is the old Gothic for 'wheel', so at Yuletide nature's wheel comes full circle and farmers await the lengthening days and the return of the sun's warmth in spring.

The yule log we burn at Christmas is more likely to be the elm log, but I remember a Christmas on a mountain farm in the Savoy Alps before the war when the yule log turned up in the shape of a delicious cake called *bouche de noel*. Or was that in Provence the year before or the year after? Christmases fly past like telegraph poles seen from an express train, the older one gets, but I still remember, halfway through our breakfast of soup and cheese on that mountain farm, how the upper half of a stable door opened at the end of that simple kitchen, and I found myself greeting a cow on Christmas morning.

123

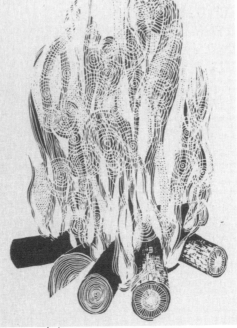

'Beech logs for Christmas time . . .'

Elm unfortunately seldom burns well, and the best of all for Christmas is ash, and then beech or really dry hawthorn. There is an old rhyme that tells you all you need to know about Christmas log fires:

> Oak logs will warm you well
> If they're old and dry.
> Larch logs like pinewood smell,
> But the sparks will fly.
> Beech logs for Christmas time,
> Yew logs heat well.
> 'Scotch' logs it is crime
> For anyone to sell.

124

Birch logs will burn too fast,
Chestnut scarce at all.
Hawthorn logs are good to last
If you cut them in the fall.
Holly logs will burn like wax,
You should burn them green.
Elm logs like smouldering flax,
No flames to be seen.
Pear logs and apple logs
They will scent your room.
Cherry logs across the dogs
Will smell like flowers in bloom.
But ash logs all smooth and grey,
Burn them green and old;
Buy up all that come your way,
They're worth their weight in gold.

A Christmas Conspiracy

GEORGE ELIOT

This second contribution from the works of George Eliot comes from Brother Jacob *and is set in the village of*

125

· A Warwickshire Christmas ·

Grimworth — another fictional community based on a Warwickshire prototype — where the womenfolk, accustomed to many years of drudgery preparing meals for their husbands and families, were suddenly confronted by the temptation of the ready-made culinary delights of Mr Edward Freely's new confectionery and pastry shop. One by one they surreptitiously succumbed to his blandishments, but the first to do so, as Christmas approached, was Mrs Steene, the wife of the coarse and ill-tempered village vet.

This brutal man had invited a supper-party for Christmas Eve, when he would expect to see mince pies on the table. Mrs Steene had prepared her mincemeat, and had devoted much butter, fine flour, and labour, to the making of a batch of pies in the morning; but they proved to be so very heavy when they came out of the oven, that she could only think with trembling of the moment when her husband should catch sight of them on the supper-table. He would storm at her, she was certain; and before all the company; and then she should never help crying: it was so dreadful to think she had come to that.

Suddenly the thought darted through her mind that *this once* she might send for a dish of mince pies from Freely's: she knew he had some. But what was to become of the eighteen heavy mince pies? Oh, it was no use thinking about that; it was very expensive – indeed, making mince pies at all was a great expense, when they were not sure to turn out well: it would be much better to buy them ready-made. You paid a little more for them, but there was no risk of waste.

Such was the sophistry with which this misguided young woman – enough. Mrs Steene sent for the mince pies, and, I am grieved to add, garbled her household accounts in order to conceal the fact from her husband. This was the second step in a downward course, all owing to a young woman's being out of

126

· A Warwickshire Christmas ·

Mary Ann Evans, Warwickshire's celebrated Victorian
novelist who wrote under the name of George Eliot

harmony with her circumstances, and being subject to claims from a veterinary surgeon fond of mince pies.

The third step was to harden herself by telling the fact of the bought mince pies to her intimate friend Mrs Mole, who had already guessed it, and who subsequently encouraged herself in buying a mould of jelly, instead of exerting her own skill, by the reflection that 'other people' did the same sort of thing. The infection spread; soon there was a party or clique in Grimworth on the side of 'buying at Freely's'; and many husbands, kept for some time in the dark on this point, innocently swallowed at two mouthfuls a tart on which they were paying a profit of a hundred per cent, and as innocently encouraged a fatal disingenuousness in the partners of their bosoms by praising the pastry.

Others, more keen sighted, winked at the too frequent presentation on washing-days, and at impromptu suppers, of superior spiced beef, which flattered their palates more than the cold remnants they had formerly been contented with.

Every housewife who had once 'bought at Freely's' felt a secret joy when she detected a similar perversion in her neighbour's practice, and soon only two or three old-fashioned mistresses of families held out in their protest against the growing demoralization, saying to their neighbours who came to sup with them, 'I can't offer you Freely's beef, or Freely's cheese-cakes: everything in our house is home-made; I'm afraid you'll hardly have any appetite for our plain pastry'.

The doctor, whose cook was not satisfactory, the curate, who kept no cook, and the mining agent, who as a great *bon vivant*, even began to rely on Freely for the greater part of their dinner, when they wished to give an entertainment of some brilliancy. In short, the business of manufacturing the more fanciful viands was fast passing out of the hands of maids and matrons in private families, and was becoming the work of a special commercial organ.

I am not ignorant that this sort of thing is called the inevitable course of civilization, division of labour, and so forth, and that the maids and matrons may be said to have had their hands set free from cookery to add to the wealth of society in some other way.

Only it happened at Grimworth, which, to be sure, was a low place, that the maids and matrons could do nothing with their hands at all better than cooking: not even those who had always made heavy cakes and leathery pastry. And so it came to pass, that the progress of civilization at Grimworth was not otherwise apparent than in the impoverishment of men, the gossiping idleness of women, and the heightening prosperity of Mr Edward Freely.

Time for Pantomime

ARTHUR ASKEY

That great Midland man of the theatre, Derek Salberg, whose name, like that of his father, Leon, is indelibly linked with Birmingham's famous Alexandra Theatre –

129

the 'Alex' — wrote in 1981 a vivid account of the British pantomime scene which he called Once Upon a Pantomime. *His choice of writer for the foreword inevitably fell upon one of the best-known comic performers of all time, Arthur Askey, whose love of the traditional Christmas pantomime was only matched by his high regard for the old 'Alex'.*

'The year war broke out' (shades of dear old Robb Wilton), I had just become a 'star' thanks to *Band Wagon* on the radio. I was inundated with offers for pantomime and eventually decided that as Birmingham was such an important city I would settle for *Jack and Jill* at the old Prince of Wales Theatre. There were at least six other pantomimes in and around the city — in fact the list of artistes involved read rather like *Who's Who in Pantomime*.

We all opened, as usual, just before Christmas, and on New Year's Eve, which was on a Sunday, we organized a 'get-together' at the Queen's Hotel where we had a meal and all told each other how well we were doing — the usual orgy of show-biz chat.

We had, of course, already heard from the paying customers that 'Yours is the best', but the name of the Alex seemed to crop up a great deal of the time and I — fresh from concert-parties and masonics — sensed there seemed to be something special about the place.

Anyway, we had very long runs in pantomimes in those days and one of the social highlights of the week was a little party given by Derek Salberg and his delightful wife Joan every Friday night back-stage in 'The Office', as it was known throughout the profession. Artistes from all the different theatres were invited and I soon became a regular 'free-loader' and began to realize what a marvellous atmosphere the place had. The building itself was everything a real theatre should

be both front and back-stage. There was a wonderful family-feeling in the management which permeated right through the staff, and I frankly fell in love with the whole set-up. I decided then and there that some time in the future I must do a pantomime at the Alex.

Years went by and I played in Birmingham dozens of times in pantomimes, revues, farces, music hall bills – but always at the Prince of Wales, the Theatre Royal or the Hippodrome, and never the Alex, apart from the odd charity show on a Sunday or a midweek matinée.

I was now getting worried. 'Will I ever do a pantomime here? Don't the Salbergs like me? (impossible). Was it something I'd said?'

In his last year of management, I played for Derek in a very happy pantomime at Bournemouth, but I still hadn't played the Alex. Then, at last, it happened. I was booked for *Jack and the Beanstalk* in 1978, but alas, by this time Derek Salberg was no longer involved in the running of the theatre, either having made a fortune or deciding to become an author instead of coping with the ever-increasing problems facing theatres throughout the country. Fortunately our pantomime did marvellous business, so my one and only involvement with the dear old Alex was a very happy one. There was just that personal Salberg Management that was missing.

I am willing to gamble that any professional performer – whether 'straight' or 'my lot' – if asked to name their six favourite theatres in the British Isles would definitely include the Alex, and you can count me in on that.

So to The Alexandra Theatre, Birmingham – coupled with the name of the Salberg family – may I say 'I thank you'.

Derek Salberg added this note to the end of Arthur Askey's foreword:

There was but one reason why Arthur, who I rank amongst the greatest of all pantomime performers, only played once for me. He was so much in demand (especially for the London Palladium) that he was never available.

from

Fragrant the Fertile Earth

AUBREY SEYMOUR

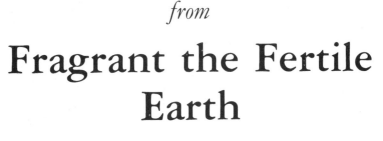

Farmer, sportsman and naturalist, Aubrey Seymour enjoyed a close affinity with the countryside, especially the rolling acres of south Warwickshire where he lived, not far from the Weston Park estate near Shipston-on-Stour. In his first book, The Land Where I Belong, *he recounted his life as a farmer through six decades. He followed this, when well into his eighties, with* Fragrant the Fertile Earth, *an evocative month-by-month chronicle of the country life he knew and loved, from which this Christmas chapter is taken.*

Christmas is the dominant theme for December, so when I heard the 'Chalk! Chalk! Chalk!' of a domestic hen turkey

'The farmer who rides *must* go to the meet . . .' Stoneleigh
Abbey provides an impressive background to this traditional
hunting scene

coming from the direction of Weston Shrubbery, it was natural
I should think that Baldwin, who had the gardens there, had
bought his Christmas dinner in advance and was fattening it
himself. I heard the call again on several occasions. One
morning it came from my rickyard and supposing that the
all-important bird had got out and was paying me a visit, I
went to investigate, but found nothing. Several days later the
harsh unmistakable monotonous note was coming from my
orchard and, determined to get to the bottom of the mystery, I
carefully crept from tree to tree. There was a final 'Chalk!
Chalk!' and a carrion crow flew off from the very tree under
which I was standing.

It was with Christmas dinners in mind that in the Earl of
Camperdown's time the big shoot of the year was held at
Weston Heath. On that day every man on the estate turned out

to beat, whether he liked it or not, and there were some in each class. A few emphasized each beat of their sticks with 'Alley! Alley! Alley!', a corruption of the French 'Allez!' and a much more effective shout than 'Go! Go! Go!' or 'Get up!' I remember one beater, a bit of a shirker, coming up to a thicket into which several pheasants had run. He stopped for a second, looked at it and walked round it with, 'Not for you, Tommy! Not for you!'

On the day of the Heath shoot we did not follow our usual practice of each bringing his own sandwiches. Lunch was provided at Molly's Lodge and drinks were sent down from the Earl's cellar, whisky fifty years old, and ginger wine of equal age that had been made by his lordship's Scottish housekeeper, and was, I suspect, not wholly free from alcohol.

The bottles looked very much alike and on one occasion got mixed. I was, as I still am, practically a teetotaller and when I tasted what I thought was ginger wine, I remember saying to myself, 'Bother! they've come to the end of the housekeeper's brew'. One of the tenants, not as green as I was, poured himself a drink from the other bottle; he came out with a disgusted, 'This isn't whisky!' and reached for the one from which I had helped myself. The youngest member of the party, the agent's son, still in his early teens, had followed my example and filled his glass from the 'ginger wine', and when we came out into the fresh, frosty air he took a header from the Lodge steps into a snow-drift. As for myself, I was too fuddled to hit a haystack for the next half hour.

As ours is a fashionable fox-hunting country, we never made any huge bags, to justify what the father of all shooting men, Colonel Peter Hawker, called a 'butcher's halloo!' Whether the sport be good or bad depends on your expectations. If you think the bag will be twenty head and you double it, everyone is pleased; but should it be the other way about, it is natural to be disappointed.

And now, at the darkest period in the whole cycle of the year, come the Christmas holidays, but let no farmer think that Christmas Day is going to be a time for lying long abed and taking his ease. Where there is livestock he is likely to be busier than usual, as his staff will expect to be off duty, and he finds himself left to do all the work alone.

Boxing Day is another matter. Then all the necessary work with the stock is done early in the morning, or after dusk, and the farmer who rides *must* go to the meet of the local hounds, while those who prefer a gun to a horse are out in the coverts after some of the old cock pheasants that have escaped earlier shoots.

Many hunt subscribers and supporters take the opportunity of the Boxing Day meet to thank the huntsman for the sport he has shown them earlier in the season and give him a Christmas box.

On one such occasion, Billy Bloor, the then huntsman to the Warwickshire, annoyed one of the keen young followers by drawing covert after covert and letting several foxes get away without putting hounds on them. When the exasperated youth, mad for a gallop, cried 'Why the hell don't you let them go?', he was told, 'You wouldn't if you'd fifty golden sovereigns jingling about in your breeches pocket!'

The Heythrop showed their appreciation in less weighty form when they presented a retiring huntsman, Sturman, with a cheque for over a thousand pounds at a meet at Moreton-in-Marsh, this being a guinea for every fox killed during his long service. An old woman among the bystanders was heard to exclaim, 'A thousand pounds! Why, old Tom' – and she named the local vulpicide – 'has shot a lot more than that for nothing!'

Personally, I was more interested in the Boxing Day shoot than the meet. It was often the first occasion that a lad was allowed to carry a gun with a party, and before myxomatosis

decimated the wild rabbits, it was looked forward to in some quarters as the one day in the year for a bit of sport.

I remember that when I was a boy, several Leamington policemen came to my father's place complete with ferrets, nets, grafts and beer, for their annual outing. I knew them very well by sight, but I could not recognize them in mufti, although one of them, named Savage, was almost an albino. They became nearly human in their old tweeds and I think I could have got away with anything short of murder for the next few weeks.

Following Boxing Day the poulterers and butchers' shops would be full of rabbits and, if the weather had been wintry, they were paunched and the flanks pegged back to show the fat round the kidneys, and prove to a shivering public that here was a warming article of diet and a bit of a change from expensive Christmas fare.

Rabbits put on weight in frosty weather and their fur also improves, but if the country is buried in snow for any length of time they will gnaw the bark of trees and shrubs and it is not only, as Tegne wrote, that 'his flesh turns yellow and becomes an unsavoury dish', but 'if he has been gnawing laburnum, he may become poisonous'.

· *A Warwickshire Christmas* ·

The snow scenes of Christmas cards rarely occur in real life,
but when they do, they are memorable – like this one near
Earlswood

137

An Armscote Carol

Nowadays, the familiar carols we sing at Christmas have a universal appeal which is perpetuated to a large extent by radio and television. But in centuries gone by, many carols, some quite obscure, were often confined to localities, being handed down from generation to generation. In 1859 in the south Warwickshire village of Armscote for instance, a certain Mrs Plum sang this delightful carol which, interestingly, contains two Saxon words, 'sensis' and 'throstened'.

There was a star in David's land,
Did in David's land appear,
And in King Herod's chamber
So bright it did shine there.
The Wise Men they soon spied it
And told the King on high
That a Prince's babe was born that night
No King should e'er destroy.

If this be truth, King Herod said,
That thou hast told to me,
The roasted cock that lies in the dish
Shall crow full sensis three.
Oh, the cock soon throstened and feathered well
By the work of God's own hand,
And he did crow full sensis three,
In the dish where he did stand.

Robin Redbreast

AMANDA RANDALL

*The Warwickshire Nature Conservation Trust is a
dedicated body whose aims are to preserve the county's
natural places and to conserve the wildlife – both flora and
fauna – with which the folk of the county share their rural
and urban environment. Dr Amanda Randall, who has
recorded these thoughts about the Christmas robin, is one of
the Trust's voluntary supporters.*

> The north wind doth blow
> And we shall have snow,
> And what will the robin do then,
> Poor thing?
>
> He will sleep in the barn
> To keep himself warm,
> And hide his head under his wing,
> Poor thing.

The robin must be one of our favourite birds – indeed in 1960
it was declared Britain's national bird. Robins feature in a
whole range of legends and nursery rhymes, such as 'Who
Killed Cock Robin?', some of which may have more than a
grain of truth in them.

One thing is for sure; most of us provide homes for a great
many robins during the festive season. Robins have become a

The robin, subject of countless Christmas cards and a
familiar friend in a winter garden

traditional feature of Christmas cards, a habit which stems
from the middle of the last century when commercially printed
cards first began to be produced. At that time, a postman's
uniform was a bright red coat, and postmen were nicknamed
redbreasts or robins. Early cards depicted robins carrying
letters bearing seasonal messages in their beaks or knocking at
doors. These jolly birds represented the postman delivering
the Christmas mail.

An old French legend has more Christian associations with
the robin. It is said that he acquired his red breast when he was
pierced by a thorn from Christ's crown. Other more pagan
ideas suggest that robins embody good spirits.

Wassailers believed that the presence of these birds in their
orchards would be a good omen, and that they would bring a
rich crop of apples in the following year. Thus when the cider
orchards were wassailed at the beginning of the year, a piece of
toast dipped in cider was poked among the branches to
encourage the robins to stay.

· A Warwickshire Christmas ·

The robin is one of the few birds whose song can be heard all the year round. By singing from specially selected song posts, robins are able to maintain their territories throughout the year, something which other species of garden birds do not do. These territories are fiercely guarded, and robins can be very aggressive towards one another, engaging in frenzied territorial battles. Experiments have shown that a robin will attack just a bunch of red feathers if they are placed within his territory! Even the Romans recorded the saying that 'a single bush cannot harbour two robins'.

Territories provide a place in which to breed, and robins start choosing their mates around Christmas, although breeding will not occur until March. Robins are opportunists, and although they will usually nest in secretive holes in tree stumps or banks, they may also be found nesting in flower pots and old watering cans in sheds or greenhouses. They will happily use open-fronted nest boxes, too, and Christmas is a good time of year to construct these. They must be sited fairly low down (about five feet from the ground) and partially hidden by plants like ivy, clematis or honeysuckle. One pair of robins may use the same box two or even three times during a single breeding season.

In gardens, robins are traditionally associated with spades and digging. A spade handle provides the ideal perch from which to spot leather jackets and other tasty insects unearthed by the digger, making the robin a real gardener's friend.

The robin's tameness with man is by no means a modern phenomenon. There are records dating from the sixteenth century of robins coming into houses during the winter to look for food. Perhaps because of their tameness, robins have traditionally been protected from persecution. An old saying runs: 'He that hurts robin or wren will never prosper, boy or man'. Nowadays, robins are protected by law.

A Ghost or Two

FRANCES O'SHAUGHNESSY

*Christmas, traditionally, has always been a time for
ghost stories, and Warwickshire has more than its fair
share, as Frances O'Shaughnessy has recalled.*

Warwickshire folk are proud of their ghosts. There is hardly a
town or village without a good ghost story and some boast
several.

Under the shadow of Warwick Castle's walls is Castle Street,
where the old timbered house of Thomas Oken still stands. A
wealthy merchant, he left generous charities to Warwick. His
house is now the famous Doll Museum and is practically
unaltered, except that the floor is slightly lower and so the
stairs have one more step. Sometimes Thomas Oken's ghostly
footsteps can be heard coming down the stairs, but they always
stop on the *last but one.*

At Coughton Court near Alcester, eerie footsteps take a
much longer stroll. They come up the main staircase, through
the drawing room and up into the south-west turret. In 1795,
Sir Robert Throckmorton filled up the moat, and tidied up the
ruins of the east wing which had suffered during the Civil War
siege of the building. He thought he'd tidy up the ghost too,
and had his workmen pull up the floor of the haunted turret.
They found under the boards a sword that had belonged to Sir
Francis Smith, rescuer of the King's Standard in the Battle of
Edgehill.

· A Warwickshire Christmas ·

Edgehill's ghosts are so famous that almost every year the battlefield area becomes a hunting ground for various hopeful psychical research groups. The impetuous dash of Prince Rupert and his troops into Kineton where they tried to capture the Parliamentarians' baggage waggons, and his delayed return into the centre of the fighting has never been forgotten. Of course, it is his ghost that haunts the scene nowadays.

The first time was at Christmas 1642, just after the battle itself. Shepherds swore that they had seen the whole battle re-enacted, complete with sound effects. Officers fetched from the King's headquarters at Oxford saw the same phenomenon and even recognized some of their dead friends. On several subsequent anniversaries of the battle, villagers in Kineton woke up in the middle of the night, and looking out of their windows on hearing screams and clashes of swords, saw similar scenes. Once the vicar took a statement about it to a J.P. who witnessed all the signatures and accepted it as a true statement of fact.

But over the years these ghostly activities have dwindled down to just Rupert's ghost dashing across the hills on his white horse. Sometimes it's his horse alone; sometimes it's his pet white dog. In 1952 the baker's boy from Gaydon saw two cloaked and hooded figures carrying lanterns and leading a large dog. They floated aross the handlebars of his bicycle in the Banbury Road near the scene of the battle. That same year the phantom horse was seen variously by local people.

In 1960 the researchers were at it again, but in spite of a generous offer by the commandant of the army camp which now occupies the site, no ghosts were discovered. (The C.O. said that any Cavaliers could be accommodated in the Officers' Mess, while the Roundheads would have to be content with the men's quarters – which shows whose side he was on!)

Of the few haunted churches in Warwickshire, the most appealing story comes from Fillongley. The altar stone was

brought here from Maxstoke Priory when Henry VIII dissolved the monasteries. People in the church have sometimes heard (but not seen) sad monks chanting the Pater Noster in Latin and have felt invisible hands trying to press them back from entering the church.

Ilmington Church has the restless spirit of a former parish clerk muttering responses up and down the aisle – mercifully at midnight, when he does not disrupt a service – while on New Year's Eve phantom hands have rung out a peal of bells to frighten away the Devil. It must be admitted, though, that neither of these happenings has been recent. An enterprising inn-keeper at Warmington, however, actually revived stories of the ghost of a singing choirboy in Warmington church in order to stimulate custom at the inn.

And the start of it all? Probably we inherit a fascination for these superstitions from the old pagan days. Warwickshire's low-lying fields and woods produced white wreaths of moving mist, often phosphorescent – which reminds one that the ghost of all ghosts was Will-o'-the-Wisp, known in many parts of the county as Hob or Hobany. At Sheldon there is Hob Lane Piece; at Copt Heath a Hobbins Close; at Olton a Hob's Moat; at Bentley Heath some meadows known as the Hobbies.

Yes, we've always liked a ghost or two around in Warwickshire at Christmastime. Look how many ghosts Shakespeare put into his plays, and he was a Warwickshire lad.

The Unexpected Spectres

RAYMOND LAMONT BROWN

Another writer who has enjoyed relating stories of War-
wickshire's ghosts at Christmastime is Raymond Lamont
Brown. In this extract from an article he wrote in 1977,
he chose spectral happenings in the county's ancient
churches as his theme.

Ask the locals for occult tales about the church of St Lawrence
at Napton-on-the-Hill, and you will be told a charming local
tale. Originally, it seems, the church was to be built on the
site of the present village green. But, goes the legend, the
stones for the church, which had been piled around the green
by the masons ready for use, were mysteriously moved
overnight to the top of the hill. This indicated, the pundits
averred, that the site for the church should be moved, and
there was the inference, too, that the building would never be
'lucky' on the green.

St Lawrence's church, with its Norman chancel, has had
many a mason work on it, and it was reputed to be haunted
long before the Victorians began their inevitable alterations. It
seems that around 1820, a visiting cleric – the Reverend
Augustus Fent – officiated for a week or two at the church
while the regular incumbent was ill.

One evening the Reverend Fent entered the church by unlocking the south door, with the object of retrieving his cassock which he had left by the altar rail earlier in the day. In his hand he carried a lantern, the flame of which – to his amazement – turned from yellow to blue as he walked down the nave.

As he approached the front pew, he noticed two women dressed in grey cloaks, kneeling as though in prayer. The Reverend Fent approached them, and as he did so, they completely disappeared – at which point too, his lantern beam assumed its original colour. How the women had obtained access to the locked church (even though the figures had disappeared before his eyes, the clergyman was too 'hard-headed' to consider them other than mortal) bothered him greatly, so he reported what he had seen to the church officers.

'So they're back again,' said one of them. 'Those are two Elizabethan ladies who are buried in the churchyard. We haven't heard tell of them for a year or two. Pity they've come back though; it stops people coming to church.'

For a few weeks thereafter, congregations were scanty – just in case the two ghostly ladies turned up too.

The parish church of St Nicholas at Alcester, its fourteenth-century tower hinting at its antiquity, stands at the junction of High Street and Church Street. Hereabouts at the turn of the century lived a lady named Livia Lee, who used to help polish the church plate. She it was who reported seeing the ghost at St Nicholas's.

Livia only saw the ghost once and no one else is on record as having seen it. Her sighting occurred one Saturday morning as she cleaned some candlesticks. Alone in the church at the time, she was replacing the gleaming candlesticks when she noticed a shadowy figure near the Greville tomb.

'Good morning,' she said cheerily. 'Come to look at our church? I'm sure . . .' She was about to say how she was sure

that the visitor would enjoy looking around, when the figure emerged from the shadow. Tall and dark with a goatee beard, he was wearing doublet and hose.

Livia's knees buckled as she fainted, for at that moment the curiously clad figure had begun to fade from the head downwards. When she came round, she found herself face down in front of the altar. Her head was against the foot of the woodwork and miraculously she was unharmed. On thinking about it later, she realized how lucky she had been not to split her head open or break her nose. Now that was strange! She remembered, as her knees weakened, it was as if someone had supported her from behind and gently lowered her to the floor.

Although she entered the church scores of times afterwards she never saw the ghost again. But she always thought that it was the shade of Sir Fulke Greville, who died in 1559 and lies buried in the church.

Set in its wooded seclusion, the church of St Michael at Baddesley Clinton near Knowle, has a ghost to add to the building's curious history. The ghost is shy, self-conscious and penitent, and is a part of the church's long tradition. The tower, the bells and the extension to the thirteenth-century nave were all paid for as an act of penance by one Nicholas Brome, who in 1517 was buried in such a place 'where people may tred uppon mee, when they com into the church'.

It seems that the irascible Nicholas Brome killed the local parish priest for flirting with his wife. It is said that Nicholas appears in ghost form on the anniversary of his death every ten or twenty years. He was seen in 1917, 1937, 1947 and in 1967 by a visitor to the church. All visitors can, of course, see what the ghost looks like, because there is a portrait of him in one of the windows.

The parish church of St Gregory at Offchurch, near Leamington Spa, is Norman in origin, and contains among its treasures an early stone coffin which it is said once contained

the body of the Saxon King Offa, legendary founder of the church. The ghost of St Gregory's, however, is anything but royal.

During the eighteenth century, a long-forgotten legend was resurrected. It appears that a man was once stabbed to death in the lane outside the church, and his murderer was supposed to have hidden in the tower. The murderer was never caught, but apparently the ghost of the victim has been seen to pass into the church and up into the tower. The murder and the subsequent hauntings originally took place around the 1650s, but in the late 1700s the hauntings started again, but with more macabre results. For the ghost would ring the church bell a week to the day and hour before anyone in Offchurch was about to die.

from

Love's Labour's Lost

WILLIAM SHAKESPEARE

The second contribution from the works of Shakespeare comes from Love's Labour's Lost. *Although set in Spain, the play ends with a song evoking the bitterness of the kind of winter Shakespeare would have known only too well in the countryside around his native Stratford-upon-Avon.*

148

· A Warwickshire Christmas ·

Like the earlier extract from As You Like It, *the Warwickshire inspiration is never far below the surface.*

When icicles hang by the wall,
And Dick the shepherd blows his nail,
And Tom bears logs into the hall,
And milk comes frozen home in pail,
When blood is nipp'd and ways be foul,
Then nightly sings the staring owl –
　　　　　To-who;
Tu-whit, to-who, a merry note,
While greasy Joan doth keel the pot.

When all aloud the wind doth blow,
And coughing drowns the parson's saw,
And birds sit brooding in the snow,
And Marion's nose looks red and raw,
When roasted crabs hiss in the bowl,
Then nightly sings the staring owl –
　　　　　To-who;
Tu-whit, to-who, a merry note,
While greasy Joan doth keel the pot.

Acknowledgements

Introductory sections are by David Green, using published and unpublished reference material and personal interviews.

The three extracts from the works of Ursula Bloom are reprinted by permission of *Warwickshire & Worcestershire Life*. *Country Calendar* by Godfrey Baseley was first published by Sidgwick & Jackson in 1975, and is quoted by permission of the author and publisher. The country diary entries are taken from *The Country Diary of an Edwardian Lady* by Edith Holden first published in 1977 by Webb & Bower/Michael Joseph (© Richard Webb Ltd, 1977). *Daisy Daisy* by Daisy England was first published by Regency Press in 1981 and the extracts are reprinted by permission of the author. 'Christmas in Edwardian Leamington' by Frances O'Shaughnessy, which first appeared in *The Leamington Spa Courier*, is reprinted from *The Leamington We Used to Know* published by the Leamington Literary Society in 1977. *Lock Keeper's Daughter* by Pat Warner was first published in 1986 by Shepperton Swan Ltd, The Clock House, Upper Halliford, Shepperton, Middlesex, and the extract is reprinted with their permission. *Warwickshire Countryside Reflections* by Roy Weeks was first published by The Roundwood Press in 1978 and the extract is reprinted by permission of Mr Anthony Weeks. 'Christmas in Ettington' is from *Beloved Warwickshire* by Mary Rose Hayfield, published by K.A.F. Brewin Books in 1983, and is reprinted with the permission of the author. Arthur Askey's pantomime reminiscences are from *Once Upon a Pantomime* (1981) by permission of the author, Derek Salberg. *Fragrant the Fertile Earth* by Aubrey Seymour was first published by The Roundwood Press

in 1970 and the extract is reprinted with acknowledgement to the author. 'Robin Redbreast' by Amanda Randall was first published in *Warwickshire, The County Magazine* and is reprinted with acknowledgement to the author. The following items first appeared in *Warwickshire & Worcestershire Life* and are reprinted with acknowledgement to the authors: 'Christmas As it Was' by Ted Baldwin; 'Post Haste!' by Vic Rogers; 'Christmases at Coughton Court' by Charles Lines; 'Grimaldi's Last Birmingham Pantomime' by Gilbert Moore; 'Festive Fare of Yesteryear' by Charles Lines; 'The Village Shop' by Fred Archer; 'Christmas at Aston Hall' by Charles Lines; 'Christmas in the Good Old Days' by Gilbert Moore; 'Christmas Comes But Once a Year' by Fred Archer; 'Another Side to Santa Claus' by Vivian Bird; 'A Charlecote Christmas' by Sally Rowat; 'Christmas in the Beginning' by Leslie Thomas; 'A Ghost Or Two' by Frances O'Shaughnessy; 'The Unexpected Spectres' by Raymond Lamont Brown. Although considerable effort has been made to trace and contact original authors, this has not proved possible in every case. To those writers who have remained elusive, the compiler and publishers offer grateful acknowledgement for the extracts reproduced.

Picture Credits

Pages 2, 16, 39, 118, 120, 124, 140 – *Warwickshire & Worcestershire Life*. Title page and pages 14, 26, 51, 53, 60, 80, 86, 103, 107, 109, 113, 133 – Birmingham Reference Library. Pages 19, 72, 90, 99 – Warwickshire County Record Office. Pages 29, 137 – Lionel Towersey. Page 33 – Baroness Ann Twickel. Page 63 – Shakespeare engraving by Martin Droeshout, first published in the First Folio of 1623. Page 67 – Leamington Literary Society collection. Page 68 – Colebrook & Co collection. Page 83 – Warwick Castle Ltd. Page 94 – from *Berkswell 1888 to 1988* published by Simanda Press, Berkswell. Page 115 – by permission of the artist, Margaret Tarran. Page 127 – National Portrait Gallery.